Todd Miller
058 Emerson Rd.
Park Hills, Ky.

The
Weather
Tomorrow

The Weather Tomorrow

John Sacret Young

Random House
New York

Library of Congress Cataloging in Publication Data

Young, John Sacret, 1946
The weather tomorrow.
I. Title.
PS3575.0795w4   813'.54   81–40227
ISBN 0-394-52149-8 AACR2

Manufactured in the United States of America

24689753

FIRST EDITION

To
Alexander Jacobs
(1927–1979)
"many long ones"
&
Jonathan Galassi

The places we have roots, and the flavor of their light and sound and feel when things are right in these places, are the wellsprings of our serenity.

—David Brower

What profit hath a man of all his labour. . . wherein he hath laboured under the sun?

—Ecclesiastes

This story takes place in the spring and summer of 1971. With a few purposeful exceptions, geography and place and time are real.

One

The earth had moved under them: that's why they were there. A freeway extension had broken up, an overpass had tumbled, and the concrete upchuck made a jetty and a divide, a trail such as a giant mole might leave. So there was work, a fast need for extra men: them. The cars were waiting.

Even before the earthquake men had been on the job. The road was a new piece. Up ahead of them it was still in preliminary and without pavement yet. The runways of beveled dirt were dry and they blew, a Santa Ana condition.

Murphy and Blue and a crane were wrestling with girders that had lost support. The reinforced tons had bent, as if they were solder rather than steel; the tremor had had no trouble with them. They still had an anodized look, like freshly treated planks of a barn. Winched free, they were gangly and dangerous, and yet, as they swung, there was a ruptured beauty to them. Against another sky, they would have been more so. The dryness sucked out the color here, and they axled against a sere immensity.

With three-inch cable as stays, the crane's monster boom had the lines of a sloop. The girders were toys beside the crane. The heavy-equipment operator worked from the cab halfway up, below the boom, setting and, now, resetting iron. Goggled today, he had fifty tons on his hands and the power and skill to do what he wanted with it. Yet there was a floating displaced sensation aloft there, a separation from consequence, an additional high. Where Murphy and Blue wanted to be.

But they were earthbound, clearing scrap, once in a while getting the use of a lowboy tractor; taking orders. They bitched and ate dirt. Sweat carried the smog's cinder and gave them red-eye; the dryness itched their scalps. The decibel count was out of hand. The money was good (if not union good like the regulars and the state men, the other color hard hats), but Sylmar, to have to be in Sylmar, a place like Sylmar? For a month Murphy and Blue debated its lack of merits and whether it was worth it.

At lunch they would unlock Rufus' GMC and then have to wait, open the doors and windows. In the heat the cab was a swollen space, a blast furnace. The captive air would flutter free until entry was possible. It was never comfortable. The seats refused to offer less than second-degree burns. The days were all the same, and one paycheck-day Dennis said, "Enough of this shit."

They sought a bar. In a sense it had been a twenty-five-year search. They had met in such a place, Shanghai Red's in San Pedro, drawn by its renown, sure they were about to be shipped out into the Pacific. Rufus Blue, huge then and huge still, had taken on all comers and gotten a nightstick from Red for his troubles. It took several strokes to calm him down. Dennis Murphy was a normal size but for his heavy-haired hands: in fists they came close to coconuts, the forearms leaned out and long as if from the weight of carrying them. He helped roll Blue out onto Beacon Street. Back came Blue amiably. The ride to the street had been time enough for recuperation. He put up drinks and stayed till closing. Neither did get shipped out, the war ended; and neither had left Los Angeles and such days and such nights had become a way of life.

Now they fell by the closest spot and ordered Old Bushmills and Coors as chasers. The bar could have been most any other, a long mirror and tiers of bottles in nickel and fluorescent cases, a Formica strip laid on the bar like fresh blacktop. The open bottles wore metal snouts like apple stems.

"I curse Henry Ford," Rufus said after ending his drought.

He had recently let a mustache grow and handlebar, but had cut it on the freeway: too many there were also growing them. All the younger men had hairy lips and were trying dope, j and anything that a pipe would draw; of course, they still drank and hated hippies. Small independent construction crews were a different matter—their newest workers smoked j and had mustaches and beards and were former hippies.

"You wouldn't if you were Hank junior."

"Well, that's another story. I'd accept the dividends, then draw the line. No cars."

"There go the dividends."

"Well, damn."

"Of course you've never owned one."

"A couple or three, what the hell. The kid had to get his rocks off."

"I hear there're other ways."

"Means to an end."

"Wait a minute, you're right. Sex and the automobile: this is significant."

"Yawn."

"They have a basic relationship, right? Now let's market it."

"Oh, Jesus, let's hear it."

They went another round.

"I haven't got too far yet."

"Do you ever?"

"What we want to do," said Dennis, "is develop a concept."

♪ "I've heard this tune before."

Murphy always had schemes for success: "There's millions of ways to make millions."

"One will do, thanks."

"But to do it without bustin ass. To be rich tomorrow morning—without haste. Consider"—Dennis numbered with his right the fingers of his left hand—"the hula hoop, feminine hy-GENE deodorant, Tupperware"—he gave each a moment to build to the next—"the one and only automatic inflatable fucking back seat!" A big finish.

"Well," Blue said, "I think I'll keep this check here, my life savings, in my own back pocket. It's got to be safer there than in your back seat."

"You're right. Too unwieldy." But Murphy wasn't deflated. "There's a missing ingredient. We need something better. Don't you see what we're looking for is something that takes no skill to develop, no technology. Pure idea."

They were ebullient; they always talked larger than life, the way they wanted to live, and they weren't alone.

"Nine-twenty?"

"Nine-forty."

"Nine-twenty?"

"Nine-forty."

"Nine-twenty?"

"Nine-twenty."

"Ah."

Blue got in line behind the nine-twenty he had discovered, ahead of the nine-forty. Another two lines snaked outside and mingled in a concrete courtyard pitched down from the sidewalk like a storm drain. These were the cashier lines; it was money that got so many up early and waiting. The lines had slack and grave and grumpy and fine and pornographic and almost famous faces. The Hollywood Unemployment Office didn't single out types. The lines began at eight and ended at four-thirty and began at eight again.

But this was Hollywood. The many performers of all kinds arrived in full plumage (a nine o'clock ahead of Blue wore skirt and blouse barely there and boots to the knee. She had pop eyes and nipples like pencil erasers). They dressed as if they were on call, prospecting. There was the money and there was nothing else to do, and the coming could produce an encounter, a job, someone to make or roll. They waited, and the dawdling lines and loitering hardship were charged with dream and lubricity.

Blue's name was called here and there—hey, what's happening?—other stuntmen, barflies and drifters, and a selection of the ladies from his life. The unemployment office was also a place to see acquaintances. There was, too, the real danger he could see some of those he didn't want to. But like the others, he waited for something that *might* happen. For him it wasn't just the fantasy and boredom of the line (and the cash in largest denominations only, the way the state paid then). He believed in where he was: action came to him, whether because of size or personality or circumstance, and he let it.

But it didn't come today.

Later Blue found Murphy celebrating St. Patrick's Day a month late at Tom Bergin's. He intentionally missed the correct date. March 17th Tom Bergin's was jammed with pink faces and expanding brogues, the mick within coming out. The ebullience there then was because of heritage, what Murphy and Blue (and many others) had landed in the southland to escape. Their own was constitutional. Purposefully so, the way they were loosely alcoholic. The liquor they drank was as much for liquid as for proof. It wasn't simply a means of further escape. The act itself, a glass, an ounce or two, the hand to the mouth, was what they knew, the background they had brought with them. They drank, and often they would get drunk every night for a while and then quit a night, a month, two, three, then binge again; and once a year a month late they came to celebrate the mick in Murphy not coming out.

Bergin's had dark wood walls and good Irish coffee, and Murphy had had one spectacular evening there wrist wrestling. Wrist wrestling isn't quite arm wrestling, it's too quick. Strength and size and weight don't have time to gather maximum effect. There's no duration, the start's usually the finish. Find braced seating, give legs stanchions to wrap around, move the shoulder in, keep a V between biceps and forearm and chin above knuckles and knuckles above opponent's knuckles—the body lines up behind arm and hand and quickness of wrist. Readiness and leverage are the greatest requirements: the pop, the snap. The wrist leads and has whip, a piggyback effect. It drives and cranks all the force and weight accumulated. Even in defense it is crucial. The wrist has a locking point, where it can hold off and hang on, and a breaking point. There's defeat beyond there; don't let a hand turn in against you.

Murphy's hands were strong, from inherited size and heavy use. They absorbed him, their singularity and a tic from an injury. Some tendons had been sliced, some minor mobility never regained. He worked his hands to rehabilitate them. They ached and stiffened if he didn't, and he learned about them. He got so he could move middle and third fingers by themselves, the others didn't even quiver; in hand span he gained an eleventh piano key. Hands were for him a form of punctuation; and when words failed, a part of speech. The wrist wrestling was a hobbied skill, the way other similar hands might have wood-carved. Wrist-wrestling contests were suddenly exploding from bar side to a sport with championships and hoopla. Murphy shied away from them—they went counter to his enjoyment; and he knew there were better at it, if not so many. He had a match this particular night as a result of Coors and paper bags.

A man in Bergin's said, "Don't throw out paper bags, bury them. They're biodegradable."

"I'm with you," a girl said.

"Save the trees."

"I'm with you. I like trees."

"That's a different kind of tree you're talking about, Gillian," the man she was with said.

"What do you mean?"

"The ones you used to . . . hmmm . . . work with in New York."

"Oh, *those* trees."

"Save the trees," the man said.

"Not those trees. On the other hand," Gillian said, "they were the most beautiful creatures. The girl models were all so skinny and flat, but the guys, they were so beautiful. They always looked a little stiff. I knew a hundred-dollar-an-hour girl who ate them for breakfast, those that weren't fags. She used to say she did because she liked the moment when the clothes came off and she could say, *'Timber!'* "

"Don't talk about yourself in the third person," the man with her said.

"Save the trees," the original man said. He valued repetition.

"Shut up with that," another man said.

"Up you and your paper bags."

"They're biodegradable."

"Is that all there is?" Dennis asked.

The exchange had him wondering: there are many kinds of bar conversations—flags against injustice, loneliness, anger or unhappiness; even solitary or gregarious happiness. Now, Tom Bergin's everyday crowd wasn't Murphy and Blue's, the place even ran to suits and ties, but these strangers weren't Bergin's either— people lost on their way. Two down from Murphy was another. No boisterousness there. This was an intent, silent, swift drinker concentrating upon mortality, and he didn't join in.

"Coors beer is a right-wing organization," the original man said.

"Now wait a minute," said Murphy. He was, after all, drinking one.

"Didn't you know?" the man said. "And aluminum cans don't rust, they don't return to the earth. They'll last and litter as long as the pyramids. It's a waste of an otherwise valuable metal."

"Let's get back to the beer," Dennis said. "What's wrong with it?"

"It's a heavily carbonated not bad overrated very light beer," the man said.

"I like it."

"That's your prerogative. They don't like to pay minimum wage. They don't hire minorities."

"How do you know?"

"Read the papers," the man said. "They're biodegradable."

"What do they say?"

"Coors is being sued."

"That doesn't mean anything."

"No," the man said. "The beer is brewed in Golden, Colorado. *Golden,* and the founder is *Adolph* Coors."

"What a steaming pile of horseshit," said the man who had objected before.

"Truth usually is."

Gillian said to Rufus, "You're so big."

"Beeg," he said.

She smacked her lips.

"Stop fogging up my belt buckle," Rufus said.

"Yes, Gillian," said the man with her.

"Wanta arm wrestle?" Gillian asked Blue.

Blue pointed to Murphy: "He's the arm wrestler."

"Him?"

"That's right."

She'd been kidding.

"All right, I'm game," she said.

"I don't take on ladies," Dennis said.

"She's no lady," the man with her said.

"Shutup, R.B.," said Gillian. "Let's do it for the hell of it."

◆ 11 ◆

She was tall and middle-aging and had perfect bones; she was well aware of each. "Forget sex."

"Don't ask for too much," Rufus said.

"Gotcha," said Gillian, her elbow on the bar, her arm perpendicular. "I'm ready," she said.

"It won't hurt," Dennis said.

"Confident soul, aren't you?"

Murphy let her arm stand ready alone. Then he moved his right in to see how they fit. "Do you want a book?" he asked. His forearm was longer than her own long one. "They're no rubber cups."

"What? Will it help?"

"There's a difference in leverage."

"All right," she said, and the Yellow Pages was produced. It was too much, but the Beverly Hills phone book was about right. "What am I into?" she asked.

She got comfortable and concentrated her attention and strength upon their linked arms. She set herself. The grasp of his right hand was still light on hers.

"Signal somebody," Murphy said. "Whenever you're ready."

"I'll call it," Rufus said. "I'll say go, and when I do you do. Clear?"

Gillian nodded.

Rufus finished his coffee. "Another Irish," he said.

He let the moment sit.

"Come on," Gillian said. "Come on."

Blue's coffee came and he sipped it. "That's good."

"Go," he said softly.

"What happened?" Gillian said then, and retrieved and rubbed her fallen arm.

When Murphy and Blue came out of Bergin's, people were all over Fairfax Avenue and a tiny Honda was turned around backwards. It was rear end in toward the parked car it had hit with its front end. From its angle of rest, there was no easy way to tell what had happened. There was a flap in the Honda's windshield—it was torn open down the middle. The safety in the glass held the rest together in bite-size pieces like set type. There was candy in the back seat along with some glass and Reese peanut butter cups on the road. The injured parked car was an old Continental.

The first passenger Blue reached kept sitting down and standing up again, trying to walk. He laid her down at once in the angle between the cars. His size made the swiftness with which he moved seem languid. Blue got her feet up on the curb, higher than the rest of her, suspecting shock, and his shirt off and under her. She wore a T-shirt that left her midriff bare, like a hot-weather football jersey. Her nose wasn't right, blue and grey. Blood on her clothes made dark droppings.

"What's your name?" Rufus asked.

"Hi," she said.

"What's your name?"

"Am I standing up?"

He wrapped the shirt around her. He wanted to get her feet higher still, but he could see no immediate way to do it.

"I was trying to walk, wasn't I?" she said.

"You sure were. What's your name?"

"Charlene."

"Hi, Charlene. How old are you?"

"Thirteen."

"You're just fine," Rufus said. "Just lie low a minute or two."

He got up, and down the street he could see the other onlookers and Murphy with a second woman.

"*I'm* fine," that woman was saying to Murphy when Blue reached them. "I'm fine. Are my boys all right?"

"They're all right," Murphy said, and Rufus looked around to see. The boys were beyond but next to her.

"I'm fine," the woman said. "Are my boys all right? Tell me the truth. I'm fine."

One boy was crying.

"Are you okay?" Rufus asked him.

"My shoulder hurts," the boy said, and he tried to move it.

"Don't move it," Rufus said.

The boy kept trying and trying to touch it with his other arm.

"Let it be," Rufus said, and he used his fingers instead, gently, like a safecracker feeling for tumblers. There were no compound fractures.

The second boy, a little bigger, a little stouter, maybe nine, stared. He wiped some tears away with his fists and stared some more.

Dennis came back and covered their legs with a blanket from the doghouse of the GMC; a second he took to the woman. He was tucking in her legs when he felt his shirt rip up the back. Blue's work. His own shirt already in use, Blue had a section of Murphy's before Dennis could register more than surprise: "Just take the shirt off my back."

"Glad to oblige."

"The shirt off my back," Murphy said again in mock astonishment.

"Put it on my tab," Rufus said.

Neither stopped moving as they spoke.

The woman was missing an eye before Blue began to wipe her face with the piece of shirt, running makeup and running blood. So much blood, but blood can fool: it can mean everything or little.

"What about my boys?" she asked.

Blue's hands shook as he worked. He asked, "What's your name?"

"Jeannie."

"Ah. Good."

"I'm fine," she said.

"Where do you hurt?"

The swabbing made her look better and it located the cuts. There was a deep clotting cut on the brow and two smaller cuts beneath the eye. There was a cut near the chin and one in the cleft. It was her face that must have made the flap in the windshield.

"I'm fine," she said.

"Where do you hurt?"

"What about my boys?"

Blue got behind her, talked close to her ear. "Take a deep breath. Now hold it. Where does it hurt?" He felt along her rib cage.

"I'm fine," she said.

Her questions didn't change, answers didn't register, she was still asking when the fire department rescue squad arrived and displaced Blue and Murphy. After checking her themselves, the paramedics hustled her carefully into the rescue squad. They also flipped out a piece of muslin shaped into a triangle, like a small folded flag, and whipped it into a sling for the boy with the hurting shoulder.

The police arrived and began to take names and ask what had happened. One cop set a string to the outside rear wheel of the Honda; the string had a level on it and he worked the bubble toward the center. People began to break up, the street emptied, the rescue squad left.

Murphy turned to Blue: "Always a pleasure to work with you, Doctor."

"Thank you, Nurse."

The last to leave, Bergin's forgotten, they sat down on the curb near where the thirteen-year-old's shoes had set, and, quickly, the exhilaration they had felt from helping began to fade. It didn't just depart, sorrow took it over. Charlene, Jeannie and two boys who were up very late—they felt like minor shareholders in these lives, and now, without choosing it, left out. They were unused to such a state and baffled by its feelings. So they sat, the sky and street dirty and lambent around them. Only the Honda remained waiting for a tow truck.

Before morning they did some laundry, Blue's shirt and Murphy's full navy bag, his entire supply of clothes. The machines were empty. A cardboard sign stood on a raised lid, OUT OF ORDER; otherwise they had their selection. This late the enamel and wattage hurt the eyes and head, a walloping light. The scuffs of careless use exaggerated. Lint drifted back and forth across the floor like tumbleweed. But there was the tang of detergents in the air, the smell of clean laundry. They needed a little fluff and fold.

Blue liked to come Sunday mornings. The girls from the nearby massage parlors came then before their day's work, laundry stuffed under an arm, a child often under the other. Young and not young, they were thin and whippy girls with no tits or lots, gentle and foul-mouthed. They found the laundromat and the mornings company against loneliness. Given the chance, they'd talk, unspooling their lives and laments, letting their kinks and naturalness out, and they'd offer in return what they considered the most they had, their services at discount.

Blue and Murphy put their laundry in and crossed the street to the Copper Penny to wait. The food there was the worst there was; even the ice water was dangerous. There was a new waitress who wore a whispery black uniform (she was the only one who did), and had black eyes and braids of black hair rolled up on her head—all her possible parts but her skin matched the coffee she poured. The hour and their condition added chiaroscuro to her grave waitress-wasted mystery. Rufus was very ready to fall hopelessly in love, and began to woo her. She would have no part of it. She ignored him and went about her business, and ignored him and poured coffee in his lap finally to cool him off when his hands found her ass. He leapt from singed parts.

"Now look what I've done," she said. "So sorry."

"There's nothing," Blue said, "like a good cup of coffee to wake you up."

"Thank you," she said.

"I love you," Rufus said.

"Oh," she said. "Will there be anything else?"

"The pain," said Rufus. "Don't you hear me?"

"I hear," she said.

"Think what it's doing to me."

"All right," she said. "I will."

She leaned over to wipe the table and her uniform whispered its secrets. Psst-pssst.

"You're enjoying this," Rufus said. "My misery."

The girl smiled. "More coffee?"

They crossed the street again, leaving a twenty-dollar tip for what she had poured; a few futures perhaps. She was still working, her grave Indian face reset. They moved the clothes into the dryers and set them going. Before they were quite dry they took them out and stuffed them into pillowcases and the navy bag. They walked from the fluorescence out into first light.

Pat wouldn't see Dennis at home. She met him on a Sunday after church, rosaries still in hand; she stowed them away when he appeared. The church had a vast triangular shell, Pup 'n' Taco magnified, glass fitted at the vertices. The boys weren't with her.

"How's the Lord?" he asked.

"Oh, He asks after you occasionally."

"Tell Him He's wasting His time."

"I think He realizes that."

"I'll bet He does and you agree with Him."

"So true."

"All my charms escape you."

"No," she said, "I admit their existence," and she smiled—her cleansed church face. Her worked-on palomino hair was as short as ever.

"What's on your mind?" he asked, irked.

Looks, and her looks, were fundamental to him: his wife was quiet, strong, at sea between thirty-five and forty and she still passed. When he had met her in his brief career as a student at L.A. Trade Tech, her body and her reserve had captured him. She had a swimmer's physique, the lifted diaphragm and deep chest (not breasts, chest), its clean strong lines and smooth face. She was firm in her skin. Touch her flesh and it thu*mmm*ed, it came back after you. Elastic stuff. A staple here, a staple there, and her body could have centerfolded. It was more than that, though: she seemed peculiarly Californian and American to him.

A part of Pat Rhodes' reserve turned out to be lack of education. Her family before her had had little school and the aloofness she carried wasn't arrogance. She was just sure of herself enough to be quiet about what she didn't know. Sudden exposure to the world—the aftermath of the war, going away to college—didn't unmoor her, and she wouldn't let Dennis touch her. Shenanigans didn't impress her. She was looking for more secure goods.

Murphy got work on a couple of John Ford westerns about 1950. They took him to Monument Valley and rubbed him up against a funning, rough but different crowd, True Believers. The time changed his life. Carrying on didn't stop, but he discovered a movie lesson: there was action and reaction, when you hit you hit someone. He became seized by a clean desire. He chased Pat to Visalia, where she had been born and her father had just died. She came to meet him at the station in a simple dark dress, her hair no longer than a man's. She wore a wide belt, a string of pearls, had a creel handbag. Murphy never forgot her there. He courted her and married her and they settled in the Valley. It paled his wildest dreams. Holding her, he could feel all that fine live packing, and the bellows blowing within. Fucking, she made a miraculous sound. He saw this low liquid vaginal squeal as the rubbings of inner flesh. More elastic stuff. Sons began popping out.

Murphy had a job managing a car wash then. In the fifties for fifty cents you hitched the car to a conveyor, nipped in to sweep and vacuum (and turned the radio on), ragged the hood and trunk a few times. The worker (and the owner if he liked) walked beside the car as soap fluff tumbled on and then off it like excelsior and the wiping strips did leisurely jigs. It was simple linear work and the mind could go where it wanted. The workers were young and sure significance lay ahead. So sure, they were loose and unconcerned and shared a rough camaraderie. Sunny times.

It was so new then, there was money to be made in the business and Murphy felt success with his small piece, and he lopped off his first twenty years, put them out of his existence. In Long Beach he had done detention on Terminal Island: intoxication, brawling, excess high spirits. He needed some maturing experience, they said, like a little time under fire. Even without it he'd done all right. The time on Terminal Island joined Chicago before it. Further loppings. He had anticipated better still ahead and sold his percentage of the one wash and stuck the gain into some lots of land.

There'd been changes since, Dennis knew: he and Blue had just worked one again awhile to turn a dollar. At a buck ninety-five now, the left-side wheels were set on a belt and the workers were black and Chicano, but for Murphy. (Rufus was a mixture he didn't talk about: a black mother, a white disappeared father whose shade he mostly took after.) To the blacks, Dennis was "our main man" or "Archie"; who knew what the Chicanos were saying? The races kept their masks in place. No ice was cut. The cars bounced from the simultaneous work of mechanical scrub and many men moving it out, but the tensions remained. The black and Chicano men wore heeled shoes beneath the coveralls and carried knives. Management let things simmer, a way to keep salaries low. Fights led to firings and made raises unnecessary. There was no reward for hard work. Soon enough the good workers saw the dead end and fucked off or moved on; there had to be better elsewhere, and before long Murphy and Blue became part of the encouraged turnover.

The customers didn't know. The wash was a diorama to them: they were sealed behind glass, with postcards and stamps and wallets for sale, soda machines for company, and a special dollar forty-nine price with a gas fill-up, fifteen gallons minimum.

Who can measure a turning point? Suddenly it was 1960 and Murphy was lurching around the house—out of work, restive, broke. He answered her silence, the dwindling funds, by picking arguments. They would end with Pat tending to a screaming Pat Jr. and him stomping out. This typical behavior infuriated him and set him off. Discipline came after the battles, but not consistently. He found work—carpenter, elevator repair, exterminator—then couldn't keep it.

She finally said it: "Can't you hold a job?"

"Sure I can."

"Well, why don't you?"

"I just never do."

"What's gonna become of you?"

"I've got ideas in the hopper."

"Oh, I've heard this before."

"They're going to happen."

"Oh sure."

"They are."

"When when when?"

"I don't believe you're saying this."

"Well, you'd better."

"What is this—some kind of threat?"

"What's gonna become of you," she said again.

He thought on that. Deeply boozed he did. He realized she said *you* not *us* and then he realized he had already become, he was. Time to dismiss the dreams and nonsense. He wasn't going to make anything of himself except to have fun while not working.

But by the time his hangover was spent, revelation had joined it. Buffalo chips. He had become an Angeleno, his one success: he had learned to make himself up as he went along. It was his failure as well: he successfully made himself over into further failures.

Now they sat in Pat's Toyota and she smoked.

"Paul's gotten into Santa Cruz," she said. "You said once you wanted to pay for it."

"I said that? This is why I get to see the queen?"

"Yes." She didn't look at him, and tried to let the tinny note of goad they both could hear pass.

"Won't Harold spring for it?"

"Quit gripin. He will. But you said."

Dennis cuffed the dash. "How come he sticks you with this piece of shit?"

Pat waited.

"What's he drivin?"

"A Datsun I think."

"The guy's a Jap. The 240Z?"

"I guess."

"Air too, right? Wouldn't you know it. What a fucker." Then he said, "Does he let Pablo drive it?"

"He's looking for something of his own."

"Like what?"

She shrugged. "I don't know cars."

"Back to my question."

"What question?" she said. "Dennis, how can it matter? What do you want, him to only use what's yours? In that case I wouldn't even be able to buy him underwear." She said, "He still has your name. So has Pat."

"Not all the Pats have."

"Well, thank God—and I do," she said.

"Blow him out your ass. The two of you together are more than I can take."

"Who's askin you to?"

"Why am I here?"

"Okay," Pat said. "Do you want to or don't you? Or shouldn't I have believed you?"

"Never believe me, honey."

"That sounds like good advice. I wish I'd taken it ten or twenty years sooner."

Dennis bow-wowed twice, kissed her cheek—she didn't react and held steady under his arm. He shook her to camouflage any soft motives.

"Open the window, your breath is awful," she said.

The Sunday morning and the car were hot, sweatworthy.

Dennis said, "How much is it going to cost?"

"The tuition's six hundred thirty-eight dollars."

"That's not so bad."

"There're the other things—living expenses, food books housing." She opened her hand to allow in others still.

"So say fifteen hundred bucks. Is that the area we're talking about?"

"In two years with Pat it could be double or triple that. If he goes to a private college, who knows."

"So five thousand then."

"Just one can be that much if it's Stanford or something."

"So thirty thousand maybe, total."

"It could be."

"Well, chickenfeed," laughed Dennis. "You know I don't have it."

Pat nodded.

"Are they doing all right? They must be."

Pat nodded.

"They're bright kids."

"My genes, of course," she said.

"The Lord works in mysterious ways."

He looked over from looking out the window. He was admiring his own wit and thinking about the money he didn't have when he realized she was crying.

For Pat there had always been the trips to Mexico, many fine times, and the last a failed attempt at recovery. They hadn't had money for a honeymoon: they had spent what they had on their house; it had cost thirteen thousand five hundred and they had put ten percent down and gotten a thirty-year mortgage at two and three-quarters percent. It was west of Studio City in the Valley in the lee of the hills; high enough so there were some trees and Pat had planted more. There was room in the yard to build a pool sometime. With it to come back to, they stepped into a 1949 Mercury with some pocket money and started driving.

The Arroyo Seco Parkway had opened and two completed sections had been torn through Cahuenga Pass. The San Fernando Valley, though, didn't have parkways, *freeways,* yet. The Murphys drove west on Ventura Boulevard to the coast and down Route 1, the way Dennis had first hitched north after reaching San Diego. The road was different then. They slept beside it or on the beach, swam before they did and first thing in the mornings. They reached Tijuana and kept on.

They stopped for *naranjadas* at the Rosarito Beach Hotel and fog rolled in. The wealthy gangstery people fled the beach and pool for the cabana bar. The fog threatened their tans a millishade and the drinking had a cheery but nasty tone; they glowered at the Bogart weather. The light scumbled. The water disappeared and then the beach, and the main body of the hotel hid in haze;

the fog crawled over its stucco sides and the bar became its own separate island. As quickly, it moved on. In twenty minutes it might never have been. They almost stayed: the hotel had a huge foyer and wonderful tile and a long, long wonderful dark wood and beaten silver dining-room bar, but the *naranjadas* weren't very good.

There was no press and fresh seethe of pit and juice. Pat loved and had grown up with fresh oranges. Her father had managed orchards and she played tag in the dusty patterns of the trees, and first thing most mornings squeezed an orange with a hand juicer made of wood and shaped like a maraca gourd. The Rosarito made their *naranjadas* from a preprepared bottle, the sugar already added. They mixed in vodka and not a light rum, and also vodka, not gin, with Galliano for Harvey Wallbangers.

The next day they found a place for them, a row of cabins along the beach just north of Ensenada. Not quite new, none quite alike, they were practically houses—with showers and kitchens and odd-shaped living rooms with oversized fireplaces and windscreened patios. They had front yards of small stones and wild nasturtiums. The stones had worn smooth and were tiered and could be ridden down a step-and-some-slide at a time to the beach. Coming in, the tide crossed the sand to hiss on the stones and suck back again, taking some with it; the stones chortled in the undertow. When the tide was high the waves broke directly on them, a part first and then another and another with a booming rapidity like artillery fire.

The water was not quite too cold. Their legs ached at first wading. The other, waiting flesh goose-bumped. But once actually in and moving, they were exhilarated before the deep cold penetrated. In the day there was the sun to warm them and in the evening the fireplace and then early sleep. They stayed several days, swimming and making love and eating heavy hand-patted tortillas and drinking the good cheap Mexican beers. They sat on the sunny, still patio and watched the whales migrate. For that number of days it was perfect; doing nothing and replenishing. Six dollars a night then. The place was named Quintas Papagayo and they came back like the whales.

Further south still, almost to the tip of Baja, near Cabo Pulmo, there was another place where the water was cool, though no longer aching. The sun penetrated it there in shafts like church light, and Pat had once seen Dennis among them, below her, swimming underwater. So short and strong—in heels she looked down on him, in barefeet they were eye to eye—he had the lines of a bullet, a bulky fish, the pads of his feet paddles and rudders, like fins—they seemed to hardly move and yet effortlessly propel —and he matched the speed of her surface crawl, and then he turned over; just like him, an underwater roll, and he was looking up at her, his eyes open, and she knew he could see her, her arms, her white suit, as bright as an oyster or the moon, and she him in the dancing nimbus, and she was sure of his thoughts right then, and her own: they were the same: one another. It was knowledge, as simple and complete as the tumble of a lock. He came up then and they swam together, on their backs, lolling arm in arm.

They never went East, never got to Europe, and Hawaii only once. They went to Mexico, and for Pat, Papagayo and the swim near Cabo Pulmo were the best parts. She didn't like Baja so much besides them, had trouble with Tijuana (the woman outside the crooked *corrida* lifting her skirt and simply squatting to pee in the parking lot). Thinking now of then, her memory seemed a sketchbook, images fixing incidentally, something here, something there. Cards that shuffled. She remembered the weather with him as much as most large events, and the events themselves broke into highlights. The pain and pleasure that came back were

like a baby's kicks while still inside. She couldn't sort emotion
free and clear from meaning, knuckle out psychology. There was
a great emphasis to—encounter groups, TA, est, the latest California dreamings. Elaborate expensive indulgent post-mortem
and lobotomy were not her sort of search of self: they stopped
her so she couldn't go on. For her despair lay in inertia.

Pat Rhodes' beliefs had been planted and pruned like her
father's citrus. They could be damaged: they had been, and she
could live with that. She cherished the elation she had felt and
the lessons she had learned. Blooms and bruises. Her harvest. All
the solutions in the swarm of belief systems she tentatively ex-
plored after the breakup of her marriage sucked at the pith of her
experience. Navel picking. Endless scrutiny, and searches for
blame. Or disposable goods. Start now, forget then. She could
not do either.

Murphy's hands, for example. Hairy monsters, and yet the way
they had touched her father's coffin, wary and wanting to, like
a builder feeling his finished work. His fingers worried the wood.
Light, loving, soothing, poignant. She knew that was too much;
fingers were fingers, not human entities. She knew, too, she was
not alone. Men seem hypnotized by exterior parts, breast and leg,
hide and haunch; women size up as well, though less directly, less
often right between the legs—yet fingers could evoke penises.
The connection wasn't precisely literal, sexual, but it was true.
In size and shape, the way they could move or set, hands offered
strength, comfort, consolation, the deepest sort of lech. Their
sensuality could be sacramental.

Murphy didn't kiss her when he got off the train for her
father's funeral. He didn't lay a hand on her there or during the
following two days. No, once—a single finger to her cheek. She
felt it still, as a fresh tear can sting like candle wax. She had
gravely accepted his coming. The depth it struck took her years

to discover and for more years it exonerated him, wiped things clean. But not forever.

There was the failure. She kept going, but the yoke of the broken marriage stuck and dipped memory into melancholy. That cast let the time of wear and tear, the hard clichés blur. She hadn't groped upon separation suddenly as if it were hung upon a single item, an insult, a physical blow, adultery. Worse than that, she thought: there just came a time when *she* had to get loose.

What else? She remembered the flying ants in her eyes. But that wasn't in Mexico. They had eaten in Sarno's after separating and he had ragged her until she walked out into the swarming ants. They had beaded the sidewalk, hopping and flying, ugly things; besides the beads, they had long jet-raked wings that splayed when they rose, and pincers. One caught in her eye. She flinched and the eye watered and blinded. She wouldn't accept Dennis' help or his suggestion (roll the lid and swim it out). The ant was like the argument inside: she took the pain and closed down around it. Dennis didn't accept her refusal.

He shoved her into the lee of a movie theater and dug after it. At his first few attempts she flinched so largely, his searching finger became a danger. He had to delicately operate. He got it out, finally. The eye had rolled it like a piece of soft, dark, obscene, morning grit.

Her eyes watered on without it. She wept because she had let herself wipe out, and from release. The struggle for the ant had let the restaurant's knots untie. He held her. Five minutes' worth of his old tenderness then.

Pat ran into Connie in the Von's parking lot. "Well, my God," she said. "Look who it is."

They both laughed and embraced, carts bumping.

Pat said, "When did you get back into town?"

"I never left. I just never come here anymore."

Amenities deflated their enthusiasm. Names were chancy: they turned over, outdated you. They were part of this trend that had become a fact, but not young enough to be easy with it. That left we-should-get-togethers and goodbyes.

Connie took her check-out slip and turned it over to jot down her phone but couldn't find pen or pencil. "Call me," she said. "I'm in the book."

Pat braved it out: "Under what name?"

"Martinez, Jack." Connie laughed. "But hurry."

Pat didn't call and then did and they decided to do it up; they went to Tail of the Cock for lunch. Both in pants, they sat in a booth along the front wall. Lunch let their talk range wider than in the parking lot. The choreography of it was to do just that: tailored pants, Scotch and white wine, the underwater light.

Pat said, "You know, you look great."

"Boy, it takes work and it saved my life. There was a period after Mr. Blue when I thought I wasn't ever going to make it back. No way. I was inta one son of a bitch after another, and then Nancy died, did you know that? She ODed in Berkeley and she's now six feet under and ashes, and whatever."

"Oh, Con."

Con: a big and brassy lady, a lapsed Jewess. Morning and night she worked herself out on a Flexastretcher. It was a musical chair. Her contortions made it squeak, sex in a sense post-Sid, Warren, Neil, Rufus, Don, Gary, pre-Jack. Weight went off with it. Now she had just given up bras and she carried them out there, sheer bravado, flex-versus-forty, and flying in the face of a latest fear, Cooper's droop. Her gait hadn't yet absorbed the weight loss; flat-footed, she still walked fat. She chain-smoked and wore its thin blue scarf about her face. Laughter leaned back her head and showed a redhead's neck. The pale pleating skin looked gelid but was anything but.

"Let's face it, I was a lousy mother. You know that: you're a good one. I'm lucky I still have the others, lucky it happened *in a way*. I woke up. So now it's marriage again and it might even work. He's fat and fifty and there's no lovin in it but there's some money and friendship. Horrors. So—"

"Check and double-check," Pat said.

"The whole Valley's probably swimmin with the likes of us."

"I wouldn't doubt it."

"Men are such shits."

Pat laughed. "They're not so bad. They're probably even necessary."

"I'm in favor of a large castration center. Balls over the doorway instead of mistletoe."

"Your bark's always been worse than your bite."

"Don't I know it. I hope now I've got an equilibrium goin."

"You still sound pretty fierce."

"It's probably seeing you. The past strikes back." She said it lightly.

"You don't see Rufus ever?"

"Zero. Zilch. *Nein.* Never. Why start that pain up all over again. He's out of my life. At last."

"Even when Nancy died?"

◆ 31 ◆

"Yes." But the word hurt her. "He cut me first." But her defense didn't help. "Okay. Okay," Con said then. "And she wasn't his child."

"He would be very surprised if he did see you. How good you look."

"That would be fun. He used to ride me. Remember I was the Pink Porkbarrel when I got second-degrees in Ensenada. I *was* a bedridden, blistering piece of red meat but he still wanted what was too hot to touch. He always wanted it, it just wasn't all he wanted." She laughed, remembering and feeling her freedom. "The grudges are gone, almost gone."

"I still see Denny. I saw him a couple of weeks ago."

"How is he?"

"The same, exactly, except older. He looks a little seedy. We're not comfortable—usually the boys are the reason we do see each other."

"He's the father, it makes a difference. And besides—as I recall, you loved him."

"There was nothing less between you and Rufus."

"Yours was . . . *gentler.*"

"Not very."

"I mean, except that he didn't grow up either."

"He got close. For a while he believed we were happy, and while he did we were."

"Maybe the four of us should never have hung out. I wonder if we could have stopped."

Pat said, "I loved learning the bad things. It made the good better."

"You were different from the rest of us cookies."

"I doubt that."

"Count the men you've slept with and multiply it by your age. I'll bet you're still short of the rest of us. You'd probably have to throw in your weight. You carried around a belief in yourself, Pat, and it was more permanent than what Denny had to offer."

Pat said, "I don't like puttin him down."

"I'm not. I'm puttin you up. Can you stand it? Let's get some coffee. Hey—"

Connie got the waiter and they stayed over coffee, cutting off their *g*'s together. There were other things in their lives to talk about besides these men.

Two

One fake fake-burning building in the Marina and Dennis at the windowless window waiting to jump, his specialty. The day was brilliant, the sea in sight and the sense of it in the air, a micalike light. Not what they wanted. They had been hoping for meteorological help and a dank day: fog as smoke's stand-in. Instead it was now being manufactured; in this case, mineral oil atomized over hot coils.

It was Dennis' first jump in over three years and not a major one. Gar, six floors up, had the real work. Murphy, halfway down, was just along for the ride. The jumps were synched and Gar, Rufus' son, had asked for him. Stunting like acting is an in thing and Murphy was out, old; he wasn't wanted. Hollywood people bear grudges until they can't tie shoelaces or they have no memories at all, depending which they need. Stunters differ; as aggressive, they celebrate their own. Gar said he couldn't do it without Murphy. Bull, but he got him. They would do the jump one and a half times, first into collapsible boxes and then a short second leap into water, the on-screen ending. The two would be cut into one.

There was a stunt coordinator: others were going to pile out under less attention. Murphy didn't know him. The fellow had an awe of accessory, Adidas Levis Gucci Pulsar. His Mercedes had the plate BOFFO 2. Dirty-blond, he wore a western-cut denim shirt and tucked the Gucci valise in the armpit so the stripes showed. Small scars ran round his mouth, fine lines like cancer

can leave. His complexion beyond them was a smooth sea of
transplant. He'd been baked a little by a flame thrower in *Battle
of the Bulge.*

Dennis got the necessary pages, not the whole script. His sole
concern was the jump. There was no school for learning how to;
you tried it and had it or you didn't; most didn't, hence special-
ization. Diving had been Murphy's start. It was the one skill he
had brought to California besides a uniform and the training to
direct an antiaircraft gun. If there had been an Olympics instead
of a war, he would have been a contender in platform diving.
It made the proximity of the Pacific seem serendipitous, yet like
everything else, he put diving behind him. He hadn't done it in
a dozen years. (Now many had trampoline training and free-fell
for fun; the confirmed lunatics tried hang gliding.)

For stuntwork, skill wasn't enough. You needed some madness
and a relationship with violence and an understanding: stunts are
not done in isolation. The camera's there. It's the mark you hit
—you're acting. Form follows function: often a fall should look
like *splat.* The coordinated, safety tuck comes at the last instant,
off-camera; or not at all.

Dennis got good at it. The danger was up to him: he plotted
it, dared it a little, teased what had never been done before. The
drive was to break new ground yet stay within performance.
Techniques advanced, costs rose; so did the danger. There were
irreducible limits, and success and injury had a physics: the more
you achieved of one, the more you pushed and chanced the other.
Stuntmen kidded it and mocked it, but it was always there in
their talk, like a deep superstition, the odds against. Preparing,
Dennis was always full of fear, and, waiting, he always had
breath-control problems. Even vertigo. Then the feel of the air.
He had dreamed of flight school and hadn't made it, and these
seconds were as close as he had come and they were the longest
and best the world had to offer. They even paid.

There came other work as well. He got shot off barroom balconies, livery roofs, off horses and by arrows in Universal westerns (flick-up arrows usually, but Dick Farnsworth let him have it once with a flaming one at a higher wage, laying it into a piece of beechwood-plus-steel taped to his chest; one stuntwoman made a living taking it in a padded boob).

Rufus Blue took spills, a spaghetti faller. He'd go down with or without horse and with little buffer, but something over the elbow and a set of baseball sliding pads. There was no live rehearsal for these, but the falls weren't haphazard. He had a mark, a role, a tested horse, equipment.

Take one: reaching his point of fall, he cleared his left foot from special falling stirrups and cast his right straight out and jerked right on the rein and the nag (and he'd better) fell left; and a double-check of the left leg to insure it was free and he began his own fall and prepared for landing. Cut.

Take two: using L-shaped step stirrups, he dumped sideways or backwards, spinning to clear the rump, and off, coming around a full revolution for the camera finish, and if to the right, the right forearm and heel usually the first shock absorbers. The ground he wanted to hit was broken up by pickax or air gun before and peat or straw camouflaged in. Collarbones were a problem.

Blue also liked the drag, the wild ride hanging by a low-set stirrup, the leg angled up as if in traction. Height helped and the angle was crucial so the head wouldn't be the only item dragging bottom. If wrong, your brains bounced out; and the animal had to be taught not to kick what was bringing up the rear. (They were mulish about learning that.) A wire ran up the dangling leg to a jacket harness, displacing the stress. It was fixed with a release. Rufus would hit it on his mark and he and the horse would part company.

In work besides westerns Murphy discovered motorcycles.

These were B movies: the bad got his finally at the hands of his own machine. They made great plot devices for the drive-in, but they were tricky to ride. You were hanging out. There was no cover, and bikes liked to catch clothing as a man jettisoned. There were bars brakes levers, a rack of interference to clear. Failure meant maiming, and even if perfectly cleared, they liked to throw and kill. Murphy knew it, yet they had a relationship to his love for jumping: they offered another sort of flight.

A visitor came over to the stunt coordinator: "Where's the show I came to see, McKay?" He was small and quick-moving and carried a leather album.

"We're ready, Jessie," the stunt coordinator said, "and now we're waiting. You know."

"I can't stay all day. I've got to go out this afternoon and get burned."

"Anything interesting?"

"A Movie of the Week." He shrugged. "We'll see what we can do. There's the shot we could get something interesting out of it."

They both stood on the balls of their feet. The stunt coordinator's hands jimmied the front pockets of his starched jeans.

"Have you seen my portfolio?" Jessie asked then. He just couldn't resist. "Mary Ann put it together for me."

He caressed the untreated pinky-tan cowhide embossed with his name, JESSIE SLINGER, and a Stuntmen's Association decal and unzipped it and inside were pictures of Slinger in flames—suited in asbestos, leaping from a car wreck, rolling in a calico dress around covered wagons; in others he dodged flames.

"How about this one?" the stunt coordinator asked.

"That was fun, but this one"—Slinger tapped himself in the calico dress; stuntmen gloried in their own tales, the jobs they had done and the closeness of the calls: they caressed the hazard, then sloughed it off, a deep pretending, more of the odds against—

"the wig was treated in paraffin and a petrol jelly for a nice smoke effect. *Definitely* inflammable. Poof. *Definitely* poof. Up it went, *my* hair with it. The Indians in the picture didn't need to scalp me. We got the shot and then they hit me with the extinguishers. Worse than the burn. It was all I could taste for three days. What I'm waiting for is this junk they're developing now. Have you heard about it? They say it can take eight hundred, *Centigrade,* up to a minute. I don't believe it but I've got to try it."

"No more of that for me," the stunt coordinator said.

"I wouldn't fool with helicopters like you do."

"They're reasonable animals."

"You should have seen what they were doing with them in Vegas on *Diamonds.*"

"Who?"

"Tibbutz."

"He's crazy."

"He was hopping helicopter to helicopter. Nothing to it."

"He's crazy, but a good man."

"I don't jump from tall buildings in a single bound either, like Blue. Gar, how the hell are you?" Slinger said as Gar came over, looking the long way up, and they slapped hands.

"What's the book?" Gar asked.

"Have you seen my portfolio?" Slinger said . . .

Today was an expensive sequence and there was press coverage. They cornered Gar Blue:

"?"

"I do it because I like it."

"?"

"I don't think. That's the worst thing you can do. I'm just going to close my eyes and go."

"?"

"Hell, yes." He ambled into a wrangler self, a stunting by-product. "I'm scared of getting my"—he offered explicatory direction—"burned off. You can bet I'll be wearing my asbestos socks and underwear up there."

"?"

"No, I'm not joking. The fire's the dangerous thing to me. We have equipment that will virtually accept a body from beyond infinity."

"??"

"There's a terminal velocity beyond which a body won't go." He grinned. "I won't reach that, I won't have time to."

"?"

"Well, I did do a little computer work at U.C.L.A. and had the trajectory checked. It's thirty-four feet down. I'll have an impact speed of just under sixty."

"?!"

"A stuntman will try anything. Once."

They fell in with him. One said, "Aren't you worried about being stopped for speeding?"

"I'll sit in any cop's lap as long as I'm able to pick up my check."

"?"

"Not enough. It never is." But he explained: "We don't have set pay scales, it depends on the degree of difficulty. We're paid by the stunt."

"?"

"This. No, this is routine, almost." He said, "I've come down from higher."

"?"

"Well, there I was at forty thousand feet and . . . "

Interviews always went about the same.

For real the prep was painstaking. Empty cardboard cartons were layered, the way bricks are laid, to pillow impact, since the men couldn't propel to the water. Two feet by four, some of the cartons had labels on them: Murphy's top tier hailed toilet paper. His rig was less high than Blue's, his jump less high. The cartons were tied in place and air bags were set on top as cushions against the cardboard corners. At sixty a corner is concrete.

Multiple cameras were placed, wide angle and long lens. They had to get all they needed in one take to separate and then link the jumps in editing, form a chase, hero after villain, Blue after Murphy.

Dennis climbed his ladder. The aluminum rang and shimmied. The going up scared him as much as the coming down. He felt the increasing altitude in teeth and balls and feet. At the top there was a ledge inside to stand on and a sill and a resin glass. There were other ladders and men around below him, background jumpers. Only Blue was above. He could see passers-by below turning into a crowd. They had no size from where he was and this had a further effect on his stomach. The fake smoke began to rise. The figures winked through it and began to disappear. He couldn't see any of them then. He was alone. He stopped thinking and feeling. He got down into himself, came up pumping; ready.

"Can you see, Dennis?" someone shouted up.

Dennis said, "Shut the fuck up."

He didn't answer the next query. He was high and violent with anticipation. All of him was waiting. That's all there was.

The cameras rolled and the stunt coordinator bullhorned the signal and Murphy aimed at the life raft of Soft-Weve.

Air.

He knew immediately he wasn't right. He was ahead of himself, too far over and on his back. Spread-eagled there was how he wanted to land, but he was turning on. He had two things to do: play his role, then save himself. Up he saw blue sky and Blue. Both seemed still. Gar's limbs were moving, though, like a letter forming itself. The moment had magnitude. The float in falling gave the arms and legs grace and weight. He felt he was waiting on their finish, a message deciphering.

Of course not. He bounced, an almost-miss. The gunnel of the air bag punched him and relaunched him. He had a second short fall off the collapsing boxes and saw stars (they actually looked more like skittish bacteria). He got up but sat down again.

"How was that?" he asked.

The stunt coordinator said, *"In-*credible."

"Applause applause applause," the assistant director said. "Didn't you hear?"

"That was fabulous," the director said. "How'd it look, camera?"

"Camera's good," the director of photography said.

"Okay here," and a thumb up from the operators.

The director said, "Print them all."

"Got it," the script supervisor said.

Murphy said, "Gee, how about just one more time."

"Ha ha," the director said. "That's funny. It was just great, Dennis. Gar unbelievable. I'll never take my feet off the ground again. From now on, it's sex standing up. Are you both okay? Great, then let's get to the finish."

The stunt coordinator said, "One or two of the lower bodies were a little off in their timing."

"Nobody'll notice as long as Gar was on."

"Right on."

"Now," Blue said when they had moved away, "what the hell were you doing?"

Dennis stayed around for lunch after he was through. The food didn't look too rotten but he couldn't eat. He was able to drink some water. His testicles hurt. Bad falls did that; the balls grabbed for the body like monkeys after a safe vine, and ached. Very much the effects of a kick there. The only visible signs of error were on his hands and knees where he had first fended off the ground, scuffed skin and a rash of dents along the palms. They wove with some memorabilia, an archipelago of small scars from a motorcycle accident. The deeper soreness wouldn't arrive until morning. There always was some pain now anyway, especially in the mornings. He leaned back in the folding chair and looked out at the water. The high-rising pokes of the Marina didn't allow much view. The catering girls began to pack up.

He wasn't alone yet. The art director was attempting to sweet-talk a girl he had gotten down to lunch from the real building; the fake front was on its way back to the studio by wide load. The girl had a nice rack. She was tiny but for them, as was her voice, and her perfect funny name buffaloed the art director:

"Bunny, Bunny Brown. How did you get that?"

"You like it?"

"I have never never heard anything better."

"It doesn't send me anywhere." Her little voice had a metallic scratch.

"Barbara, Bonnie, Beatrice, Bertha . . ."

"Bunny."

"You were born with it. Wow. People have been murdered for less."

"I doubt it."

The art director said, "I love your office, all that shag and repulsive Naugahyde. I didn't need to dress it at all. It's perfect. Do you like working for this guy Barr?"

"It doesn't send me."

"You don't want to be a secretary all your life."

"I'm not. Dena who wouldn't come is."

"She's attractive. I was hoping she would."

"She doesn't trust men."

"You do?"

"I'm not worried about it."

"Why did *you* come?"

"A free lunch. To see what was goin on."

"Not for the adventure?"

"What adventure?"

"Lunching with the stars."

"I am?"

She practiced so well without apparent training a Hollywood lesson, a secret of success, the delivery of sarcasm without inflection.

The art director wouldn't be taken aback; "If Dena's the sec, what do you do?"

"I answer the phone."

"All day?"

"I can't type."

"With your looks and talents, you must do other things."

"Oh, Mr. Barr thinks up one or two *special* assignments for me."

"Oh."

"One or two."

"I hear he's being investigated by a grand jury."

"I wouldn't know about that."

"Don't you listen when you answer the phone?"

"What?"

"Are you pulling my leg?"

"What?"

"I wish I could see behind those sunglasses. Do you have to get back soon?"

"It doesn't matter."

"I'd love to show you some rooms, what we're doing with them. They'll be filming in some. Would you like to meet Clint? I think we could swing an intro."

"Really?"

"Sure."

"How long would it take? I'm not sure I have that much time."

"Well, there's always after you're through work."

"There is?"

"Things to do . . ." he said.

Bunny put up her glasses. "I like your mind."

At last. The art director basked. "Thanks."

She looked him up and down *physically,* measuring his potentialities. "That's no compliment."

The line was one of the great ones of life. After howling, Dennis wanted to just sit and admire its levels. The art director was on his ear. With some bitching he retreated and Bunny lowered her glasses back and bit a peach, content by herself.

Dennis said, "You get off some good ones."

"They were nothing special."

He laughed: she was still fulfilling herself as a sensation, her tiny voice and big boobs, her jugular instinct. He had no particular idea of hustle; but for pained balls, he felt in the clean sweet loose drunk of aftermath.

She finished the peach, spit the pit. This canted her and upset equipoise. It blew spatial relationships. Mouth quick, body slow, she moved into another sort of space, and his muse became concupiscent.

She watched the seed traject and land. She said, "I saw your fall."

"And . . ."

"I wouldn't do it."

"But how'd it look?"

"Don't ask."

"Come on, I'm asking."

"Like a sitting duck falling."

"Thank you, thank you."

"Don't ask next time."

He sat a minute. "You're not going to ask why I do it."

"It's nothing to me."

"But it's the next question asked, you know."

"Not by this girl."

"God, you're good."

"I do my best."

"Ah shit," he said, carried away, "You are the greatest thing since the invention of the groin vault, since the development of the flying buttress, since—"

"Slow it down, son." She scolded, South as well as West in her.

"I'd like to have you answering my phone."

"That line is busy. I'll put you on HOLD."

All seats and tables up but their own; they were alone.

Dennis said, "No can do, I'm goin now."

"Oh, where to, do you think?"

"That great telephone booth in the sky."

"Aren't you satisfied? You almost made it there half an hour ago."

"I don't want to go there alone this time."

"You had that other stud."

"No studs allowed."

"Oh, can't you get it up," Bunny said.

"God, you're good."

"Such bullshit."

"I know it," he said.

"Such bullshit."

"You doubt my veracity."

"Spell it."

"Your-ass-is-grass-ity."

"In that case kiss it."

"In that case bring it on over here."

"Fat chance of that, son."

"There's no way I'm going to win this, I know it," Dennis said. "Anytime, I'm ready to concede."

"Fat chance of that, son. Look again."

He did. Her face opened around the dark glasses: she grinned. Her lips thinned à la a rubber band and her teeth flashed. They were sharp and straight and just nicotined.

"You-oo send me." she said.

Did she have some friend, a good old girl? Well, she might: meet her in Manhattan at eight o'clock.

There were slap-ups everywhere in Manhattan Beach: the correct R-3 address was on the Sand and prime, the Blue Book a block down. The apartments were pink and beige and fading avocado. Script names swam across some—Pacific Lanai, El Camino Royale, Casa de Oro, The Sounds of the Surf. Rufus' GMC was a monster here and they had to double-park. This was Porsche land. From his door Murphy used the roof of one to reach the sidewalk, a minor leap. Two mustaches in Ts and shades eyed his maneuver from a balcony, sipping Buds. They made no comment, their cool remained unscathed. Through the building stereos fought for aural space. Walking inside, Murphy and Blue felt the war even through their feet.

The girl who swung open the appropriate door looked Rufus' hunk up and down a moment. She said then:

"Seductions are in order."

"I must be in the right place," said Rufus.

"Well," the girl said, "what are you going to do about it?"

"I'm going to thoroughly investigate the situation."

"That sounds like it could take forever."

"Done," said Rufus, grabbing her.

"Now you're catching on."

Rufus to Dennis: "Where has this been all my life?"

"None of your damn business," the girl, Toni, said. "And don't waste your time with the parts of mine you'll never have."

"Jesus, am I in the right place."

"Don't let it get around," Bunny said from behind.

Toni in Rufus' light grasp was a tall girl with streaked hair. She had been KHJ-TV's weekend weather girl and had just become their weather person. The change didn't affect her salary, only the clothes she could wear. The forecast showed less of Toni than it had before, and she hadn't yet achieved the crossover into hard news. She had no anchor spot. A few women were breaking through, gaining notoriety (including requests for autographed pictures), and major dollars, but those who didn't disappeared quickly. There was possible media stardom but little middle ground.

Her job made for a recognition factor, a familiarity; she too often got the line "Haven't I seen you somewhere before?" There was also the chance they had. She got around. She was a war baby, conceived in a back seat on a last leave, a posthumous child. She got out of Toledo, where she came from, as fast as she could and wasn't going back. She had the usual skeletons: early marriage and divorce, a couple of abortions, a period of drift, a landing in Southern California; now some sudden success. Her past life was a print-out.

From the doorway they drifted into the balcony congregation; daily it grew with rush hour, diminished with dark: 'staches and shades and halters and hibachis and Bud cans between sips along the iron-rung railings. For the busy the day fell away here. They sucked the ozone and ocean air, decompressing, looking over their leisure. Mecca was to the west. The ritual was the quiet time between money and pussy.

In the GMC, Murphy and Blue and the girls drove down Highland to the Buccaneer. Rufus kept a good part of his life in the truck and they had to shuffle it to fit in. The street was sluggish, traffic and dusk. There seemed no end to rush hour. The swell was also summer numbers, kids in bikinis and cut-offs rising from the sea. They were sexed and kilned by the beach, Caucasian sights in pottery shades. With Labor Day they would seep back inland beyond Ardmore and into the Trees.

By the minute the light gave way. It didn't blaze or flame out. It didn't die with radiance. Darkness came like shade and then a smoke before you realized what it really was. Brake lights began to hue it, winking in ruby constellations, and as they could cars peeled off into side streets and stepped on it. It was Friday night.

From the Buccaneer door the bar was fifteen minutes away. Progress was single file, sidewise, bump'n run. Elbows and hands joggled glands, you couldn't help but cop feels. Waitresses struck out as rescue dogs through snow. The noise and action quaked the floor and anything less than a shout had to be repeated. The constituents adapted: there were rules inside the wildness and tensions inside the laughter. They were here to make time.

"Don't move," Rufus shouted.

"What? Who could?" Toni said, but he was gone, bumping 'n running. His fantastic size kept his head briefly afloat.

"It was nice knowing him," she said. "Hot temps tonight."

"Toni!" A man in a candy-striped polo shirt hailed and embraced her. "What's the forecast, baby? Are you coming to the party?"

"Which one?"

"Any of them, all of them."

"Hot temps tonight! I'm throwing my own."

"When do we start?"

"We're starting at Leonard's at two A.M. Do you know Leonard? I'll meet you."

"I'll be there."

He moved on.

Toni to Bunny: "Full wallet, flabby body, fat head."

"That's a dilemma, all right."

"I'll bet he shows at Leonard's."

"You mean there is such a place?"

"Would I lie?" And she was hugged again.

"Tim," she said when he left.

"Who he?"

"Drove over a pig in his Alfa Romeo. Awful thing."

"All that ham in the suspension system."

"Loved that thing."

"Like a brother."

"Waaahaaa!"

"Soooeeee!"

"Now he's a flight controller. Recently married." Toni said, "He's eager, though."

"He's married, not dead," Bunny said.

"Now who's going to be next?" Toni asked the room.

There were many possible answers.

"This is what I wanted," she said. "This is what I always wanted. Thank you, gentlemen, very much."

"But is it enough?" Bunny asked.

"Is there such a thing?" said Toni.

Rufus came back, a bottle under an arm, a waitress on his shoulders. He lowered her down.

"The only way to fly," she said.

"I would like to have had my head the other way round," Rufus said.

The waitress missed his meaning but winked as insurance. She tucked her tip strategically and began her return run.

Rufus couldn't resist going on. "I desire tunnel vision." He loved his line.

"Your head's already on backwards," said Toni. "There's a pay toll there and many have paid."

Bunny noticed Murphy's quiet and made inquiry.

"This is great," he said.

"Who, which, what?" she said.

He yelled it.

She put her lower self against his leg, crooned her tiny voice into his ear. "Don't Bogart me."

The sweet nothing informed him: as a foursome they hadn't yet knit. The lines were there and they were throwing them, but the jam interrupted. He was certainly used to noise and drink and wasn't sure why, and they stayed, a haze of smoke and body heat lifting above their heads and folding back from the ceiling onto itself and into a cloud.

Still Murphy didn't come out until they moved on, out of Manhattan to the Ballroom in Santa Monica. It had a different crowd, hippies and wild men. Here Murphy and Blue were known, shareholders in some raucous late-night events. In the early evening, like now, these were ready for retell and embroidery, on call like jukebox numbers, and quickly the girls became audience. The old professions whoring and storytelling inhabited the Ballroom, stuntman ingredients. With lopsided heads and small and large scars, like a breed apart, they had exuberant, transient sex lives stirred by competitive spirit (yet fell in love with profound, comic, soap-opera depth) and endless stories welling from brag and nerves and battles with sleep. They tended to insomnia they carried so much charge; sleep often didn't come until daylight.

The premiere story had to do with the size of the room. Once it had been small—too small it was decided one night. Claustrophobia set in. Those present took improvement upon themselves. Their method had a basis in a late-night punch-out they practiced. The chest was the target for these exchanges, no head shots and no belly or low blows allowed. Before each you had a shot of booze, your choice of poisons. The process was formal, turns

closely kept. There were rules of disorder. And from one thing
or other, somebody would go down, the loser. Redecoration
night the walls became a substitute. They weren't ply and didn't
cave easily. They repelled fists and rawed knuckles, broke one or
two. In addition, the drinks had effect. Murphy was the one who
found the necessary solution with a butt of his head. The first hole
knocked him cold. The others punched it out from there and he
woke to spit bits of plaster out and resume, and before morning
it was anything goes.

And the subject of O.K. Freddie arose, a shabby man, a drunk,
with a long loose loping walk like Groucho. He smelled people.
He tailed them on the street, slunk next to them at the bar, set
himself and ran his nose from subject's waist to head, sucking
essence. His nostrils wriggled, he savored what he got. He had
no shame about it. This had its uses to them: sic Freddie on an
unwanted bitch and you got rid of her. The legends around him
didn't end at his nose: there was his cock, a giant in the industry.
It was like a living animal, as thick as a wrist. The actual number
of inches was in dispute. Claims kept elongating. He could tie
it in a knot, it was said, then the kind of knot was debated. One
famous actress, it was said, had hired him as a waiter at a cocktail
party and he served it up, a pretty good sight gag until a woman,
without looking, stuck a fork into it. The rest of his life was a
mystery. Where did he come from, where did he go? He appeared and disappeared without pattern, and speculation became
myth. (He was soon to die, but of what, no one would know.
His time had come.)

Leroy, next to Bunny and her size, said, "He'd like you girls."
He tended to mumble and talk a sort of black Okie, a lot of pose
and strut. In his mouth girl rhymed with curl.

"Listen, bring him on," Toni said. "I once had a guy fall in
love with my armpits."

"That other guy must have had a bad sense of direction," Leroy said.

"Not so. Besides, you haven't seen them."

"Seen who?"

"Les pits."

"There's an offer."

She jerked a thumb. "The line forms at the rear."

He looked in that direction: he was a body man, a parts expert. "There's a better offer."

"Easy-steady-*big*-fella," Bunny said and everyone, except Leroy, laughed.

Murphy plunked a bill down. "Max, we need some work here."

Max filled the empty glasses.

"What is this stuff I'm putting into my body?" Toni asked.

"Pilgrim's Feet," Rufus said.

"*What?* Max, what is it? At the rate it's going down I guess I won't have to wonder long."

"Let me give you another," Max said and poured for her, the perfect bartend. "You're drinking Plymouth gin with a little bitters and my special mix."

"Nice and easy," she said. "It looks like a barber's tonic."

It was a pale green, almost milky.

"How do you know that?" Blue said.

"One of my many former careers."

"Should we ask about the others?"

"No comment," said Toni.

Max said, "It looks a little like pulque, actually."

"This is it," Murphy said, excited, "the one that's going to do it once and for all. A. New. Booze. Consider the possibilities. Bourbon—Scotch—gin—now . . ." He laid out his left hand as if it held what he hadn't yet said, an act of restraint. "Ladies and gentlemen, we need a name for our new product, a perfect handle and we're on easy street."

"Again?" said Blue.

"Just come up with it and you've got fifty percent."

"Might I suggest the product first," Rafferty said. He was another Ballroom shareholder.

"Shove the product, we're idea men. The name comes first."

"Fucking A," said Rufus.

Murphy considered seriously. "It has a ring to it." He turned to Bunny Brown: "What do you think? The label, can't you see it—one young lady"—his hands conjured her—"wrapping around the capital letter."

"They'll ban it," Rafferty said.

"That's perfect. We'll build an anticipation."

Bunny shook her head. "It sounds like a douche."

"Now you're talking," Leroy said.

"Okay, what are the sales figures there?"

Bunny said, "I think you're getting in over your head."

"All right, then, we'll have to have other suggestions. Blue?"

"Working on it."

"I think I have it," Rafferty said. "Kumquat." He pulled his beard, considering the idea, his idea, seriously now himself. "I think it has merit. Knock it about. Give it a go." In fact Canadian, he was becoming broadly English; drink did that.

"Pilgrim's Feet," Blue said.

"That's taken."

"Look, I'm just ordering."

"This is a serious business, this is no laughing matter. Titles are an art form."

"Feet First."

"That's how we're going to go out of here," said Toni.

Leroy laughed. "These are no ordinary bags. Quick."

"I have a good straight man," said Toni.

"I'm hip."

"A genius going unrecognized in his own country. Oh, the tragedy and irony of it all." Murphy said, "Max, I need your help."

Max poured.

"Max, have you ever been in love?"

"No," Max said, "I've been a bartender all my life."

"Move on down the line with that, Max," Rufus said. "We've heard it before."

Max poured.

"I say," Rafferty said, and received.

"Well, I'm in love with this little woman here." Murphy put his arm around Bunny but she wasn't there. His head spun. "Whoa," he said.

"Murphy, you have gotten what you deserve at last," Blue said. "You have gotten the gate."

"What goes on?"

"Believe me, it is the case."

"Fuck you, Blue," Murphy said.

"It's what you get for spending all that time making those millions."

"Fuck you."

"History repeats itself. I tell you, the women just don't want those millions."

"*Fuck* you."

The conversation had turned, suddenly he was worked up. He took a half-hearted, hardening swing at Rufus that never landed. Bunny popped into its trajectory but beyond: she came out of the can. He loved it, operatic, casual, his swing, her emergence. The fury went sweet. He watched her come on.

So did the others. Blue turned to see the three next to him lined and pointed, swiveled like gallery ducks.

"So sorry," Bunny said, arriving. "Dysentery, don't you know."

"I'd jump her," said Leroy.

"Don't bite what you can't chew," Blue said.

Leroy masticated.

"What'd he say?" Bunny asked.

"I was admirin your form."

"You've cotton in your mouth, son."

"You don't have to hear the words to know what he's saying," Toni said.

"I'll show you something," Leroy said. "See this."

"What?" Bunny asked.

"This." He pointed at the gap between his front teeth. "You know what that is? A clitoris slit. Put it there and you're mine. Brrrrrwwhaaaa. Hem, him, hum the Marine Hymn and you're mine for life."

"I didn't hear that," Toni said.

"Mmmmm," said Bunny, "so that's why you've been sniffin about my kneecaps."

Leroy bowed. "Higher than that."

"Okay, okay, junior, just keep your hands off my ass."

"Nice buns."

Bunny shoved Dennis back. "I've got charge."

She turned on Leroy and threw a pantied moon. The panties were black-and-white-striped: "Zebra power!"

"I can go for that," said Leroy.

She farted. "That's all you're going to get."

"Let's hear it one more time," Toni suggested.

They moved around to the Raft, the Old Place, and had Hobo steaks and tequila, and then they cut out but not far. The GMC was close and good enough. Later they drove Mulholland east to Murphy's lot where his Open Road stood. The piece was ripe for cantilevered building. He had thought that when he had bought it in 1955, *some day*. The thought and the lot remained. A pull-in was worn, succulents grew and slid and grew and the Open Road arrived and now seldom moved; in general Murphy couldn't afford it. When he had some money he fixed it up with a ball and hitch, cut in a picture window. He did the work himself and blew out the insides, gutted the motor home. He took it down to walls and left it. There were a few compromises: he moved in a leather chair, a South American hammock—a cut of comfortable cotton blanket with spidery clews—and a six-inch-thick slice of foam for the floor. There was a kapok sleeping bag beginning to lump for covers; it unzipped all the way around. In a corner there was a Toro also, a clotheshorse now, bought and used once on the grass outside that came in January and dried by May.

They climbed to the roof and contemplated the view. There were shiny skins of eucalyptus close by and concrete stubble, the underpinnings of houses that had been built. Some smoky city lights flowered the Nichols Canyon gap. They set in a green swarm like dock lights across a sound, smog's effect. Toni reached out to the vista and spread her arms and gave the weather report:

"There's rain, the map says, just about from the Rockies on to the East Coast, a big low-pressure area that's just sitting there and causing grief and the Midwest is going to get some thunderstorms. Watch out: in Indiana they're looking for hailstones the size of Christmas tree balls we're told tonight. It's going to be a rotten day most everywhere, except for right here in good old Southern California. Nothin but sunshine tomorrow. Valley people, it's going to reach a bright beautiful one hundred out there, while high desert towns can look for a hundred and five and in the low deserts it's going to be a cookin one hundred and fifteen. In Palm Springs there'll be hard-boiled eggs on the sidewalks. But it's going to be cooling upstairs tomorrow night, so watch out. The temps are going to drop, so cold it'll freeze your birdbath. Well, not quite. On the Sand look for a high of eighty degrees, and if you take the plunge, a perfect sixty-nine. And right here downtown at the Civic Center it's going to be a round nine-o. Okay. And no smog anywhere. It looks like a beautiful day. Just like every day. Have one, y'hear, you deserve it.

"Shit you do," she said, and sat down.

"No exceptions?" asked Blue.

"No, you're right," Toni said. "In 'sixty-nine it rained forty days and forty nights."

Cold began to bring down their high and they climbed down and Dennis lumbered the Open Road into activity and they drove. Soon the girls passed. Murphy and Blue sat up front. The world seemed to glide below as well as around them; in the RV they felt on top of it. They shared a number and a beer, and the driving and the drunk and the getting stoned gave a quiet rush.

"How was he?" Blue asked after a while.

"He was—fine. The kid's as good as Simmons or Jack Cooper. He shows up his old man."

"He was going to be an engineer. I don't know where that went. Now he's a fuckin stuntman."

"He engineered himself down from eight-five feet."

Rufus shook his head. "He's out of his skull."

"That's inherited."

"Well, there's still a shot a couple or three of the others will go straight."

"Thanks, Dad."

"Worse than that."

"What?"

"It turns out that son of a bitch Gail cohabitates with has balls, after all."

"Grandad!" Murphy said, "Put it there, mother." They shook right hands.

"Ah, fuck," Blue said.

They rode and Blue said, "You didn't tell me how the ride was for you."

"I pulled the string out."

"That's routine."

"No," said Dennis.

"What the hell."

But for the first time Rufus looked over. He said, "Well, *fuck.*"

They rode, coasting, but the silence wasn't rudderless; it had thoughts. They journeyed along with the road hum, then fell away, forgotten again.

At some point Murphy reached for the beer and found it gone. "How 'bout a bar and gorilla run?"

He didn't get an answer.

"I'm the only sober one in the house," he said, and drove as the others slept.

At Joshua Tree the morning came without approach. There was night and quick sudden light, no in-between. The first sunsheets immediately overexposed—by nine it was the color of bone. A hot day. Another hot day. The light penetrated apertures in the Open Road like projector throws. After peeing, Bunny opened the toilet door into one. She was a match for it, all white light. She uncramped herself and stretched in the ignited spot. Small, she looked vast.

"The plumbing around here leaves something to be desired," she said.

"Mine or yours?"

"Both this morning. Whew." Her breasts swam surprisingly low. In stretch, arm up and other out, they took an odd kilter, raised and buoyant, proverbial melon, and ovoid and falling without landing.

"When did they start growing?" Murphy asked, watching.

"When did what—? What a dumb question."

"Every gland I handle, I want to know where it comes from."

"Mine or yours?"

"Your two beauties."

"From here, son." She beat her chest Tarzanlike.

"Far out."

"They're just boobs."

"Bull—shit."

"Well, they're a lot of them hanging out these days."

"Not like that."

She looked them over. "I suppose, but they're a pain to lug around sometimes."

And she set them at ease in a light bra. The motion was a quick and dexterous forward bend and a reach behind herself. She wore a heavier one to work. She was supported then by every bony invention foundations had to offer.

She moved out of the light, and put on a pair of yellow panties. "This is my McDonald's suit. Behold the Golden Arch."

"How many of those do you keep in stock?"

"What do you mean? I always carry an extra pair of panties in my bag."

"I meant the lines that go with them."

"I can cope." She dropped them back down and profiled herself, her high low bones and the tight packing of pubic hair that covered them like a Brillo pad. "Here's the best line of all."

He had to take off his hat and pants to her, a quickie that ran on into a slow slow one. Set off by her panty shot he thought of Pat. He often did as he stepped into underwear: she had changed his habit, jockey to boxer. The sex finally teetered between pleasure and a kind of pain. They slept after combat.

In the hammock Rufus asked, "How's the weather down there?"

"Wet," Toni said.

"How's the weather now?" he said later.

"Oh, stow it," Toni said, "and take care of business."

The day passed in quanta of heat and fantasy. They never made it outside, but inside a lot: they could find double meaning anywhere. They set up a small silver hookah, later did a few lines. They drank Bohemia a little blown away.

Murphy noticed things he hadn't before. He could taste tequila salt on his left hand along the webby crevice and ovoid muscle of thumb and first finger where he couldn't flex. Nearby was a flap of skin ripped by the fall and dried now to the stiffness of a potato chip. He noticed more about Bunny's teeth. She ate enormous amounts of peanut butter and her teeth seemed a little that shade. Even with her mouth full, she laid down lines. No end to them. Some he lost to her chewing process, the peanut-buttered pronunciation, and the way her mouth itself moved. He was mesmerized by her gargantuan sensuality. Hand on her hip, too, he could reach around her iliac crest and find soft snow. All that white flesh.

Between grabfuls, the Bohemia quickly gone, he found a bottle of *vinho verde* stowed away. It was sweet, but not too, and white and Portuguese and, cooled, so good; it helped combat dehydration. The Open Road got very hot, dry heat. Prickly heat, Bunny called it. Pretty funny. Laughter had the effect of raising more sweat. "I've got a pit and three-eighths," Murphy said, and Toni bared her famous ones: a few waffles of skin and just seeded with stubble and wet. They laughed and cooked in their own juices.

At its end the day went maize and then the shade of orange juice; the harsh light disappeared in sudden tiers. Hollywood did astonishing things before sunset also, like orange juice, and someone happened to remember Toni should have been back there at work.

The Chinaman had five trucks in his private disposal service and Murphy and Blue took to driving one. The Chinaman himself didn't drive except once a week to sift artist's trash cans in Venice. He had founded a collection with their discards, and a profitable sideline. The merchandising won his provenance large canvases of enmity which he ignored. The rest of his time he spent cracking a whip: he was the asshole to be faced at the beginning and end of the day. In between they were on their own.

Quickly enough they discovered the work was boring, never-ending, the butt of jokes; the surprise was they liked it. The low status between plumbers and Polacks mattered some but was changing fast: garbagemen had become sanitation engineers besides. The profession had a growing necessity. Five and a quarter pounds were produced per capita per day, and the glut had a geometric growth pattern. Murphy and Blue shoveled against futility, doing some good. It was easy to make light of the usefulness but they felt its elation and succor. And the work was outside and got aggressions out.

The day began early, 4:30 A.M., and ended usually by noon. Sanitation uses mean machines, has to: they had to hold or eat practically everything. Few were alike; there were models and options galore. On international chassis alone—which were all rear packers and right-wheel drive—Heil or White or Masters uppers were available. Los Angeles service used all three and three others as well, a shorter truck for the twisting Hollywood hills, furniture vans by appointment only, and ten special trucks for collecting dead animals.

But Murphy and Blue's was a junk: it had no hopper and cranky hydraulics that went in and out on whim. It was a front loader and the bin rode above the cab and dumped to the rear. There were no push or sweep blades to compact what was inside. Once the truck was full, that was it. Brooms tucked behind metal joints along its sides like pencils behind ears. Many paintings, forest- and pea-greens and battleship-greys, wove into one another, mixing like camouflaging. Rust barnacled. Its ride shook the bones. An ancient machine: soon it would join its contents.

They worked the shoeboxes and trailer parks above the Pacific Coast Highway above Santa Monica. Fernwood, Rodeo Grounds, Las Tunas. They saw little of their denizens but got whiffs of personality and eccentricity: good red meat, bad red meat, toilet bowls, real silver candlesticks, a working power saw, a raccoon coat, a pharmacy, the most mysterious Rube Goldberg contraptions, filth. Lots. The people they did see tended to be in underwear, rushing out a last item. Once or twice they were offered cookies or a cold one, or a six-pack sat on a can top, and they were a hit with small children. Pint-size faces and large eyes pasted to screens and windows to watch and wave brought by one of the early recognizable sounds of their lives, the whines and grinds of the truck and its tired parts.

The curb displays were picking grounds, etiquette said, and Blue redecorated his living room accordingly. Soon enough, though, he tired of acquisition and the rarest objects received only the slightest attention as they joined the amazing, limitless inventory and were thrown in. Nothing more. Nothing fazed them. There were other reasons to let discoveries go, too: rats preceded them into the stacks, shinnying down from the palm tree where they lived; and it was easy to get lice. For several late-summer weeks fleas attached during pickups. They gathered on the heaps and rained from dry brush upon touch. They took over L.A.

While working, Murphy and Blue bounced around fifty-gallon drums. During the rainy season (when they wore yellow waders) or filled with a surprise, like plaster, these could weigh several hundred pounds. It built their arms and lats and warped their vertebrae and inspired hernias. But one thing a bin didn't do which many hoppers did—it didn't spit back what you shoved in. Still, if the heat allowed, they protected themselves with two layers of clothes, undershirts and work khakis, bandannas, hardish hats, shitkickers. The gloves with long cuffs and the aprons they wore over didn't last; they got into some remarkable smells. And even with the gloves Rufus contracted awhile a pimply infection that stacked around the knuckles like beads of tapioca.

The rubbish went up to Landfill #3 on Sepulveda Boulevard. During the week six or seven Caterpillar tractors were on the line turning it under, four thousand tons a day, five in the summer. The pads rose to the level of virgin earth, small-time orogeny. When this one was finished before the end of 1971 they would move a mile down the hill and begin another. With the per-ton fee the operation was a moneymaking concern for the county, and behind it were coming condos and a golf course. Up the Santa Monicas the first sandtrap had been cut into the last fill.

Sepulveda was the end of their day, Saturday the end of their week, except for the empty drive back to the Chinaman. Especially Saturday the public joined them there. The numbers were surprising. Banged-up pickups and El Caminos paid the toll and wound up the dirt road to unload. The drivers could be geezers in old golf hats or long-hairs. The young ones often came in groups and brought their girls; who knows why. Rufus had a favorite among these: she sat in the cab and combed her hair and sucked beer while her man emptied out his rear end. She wore her tits loose under a T with a barbell on it and her breaths bent the bar, ballooned the bells. Her expression never changed. She had a remarkable young stoniness.

They waited one Saturday for her show with a case of beer of their own. They used a battery-run fan they had rigged in the cab to breathe. Early in the morning there had been a brief freak summer rain—there was twice as much rain here as anywhere else in the county. The moment it stopped, steam rose and the color spectrum shifted. There was speed to the clearing. An hour after, the storm might never have been; no sign lingered except the several inches of mud the trucks churned up. All but two of the Cats were off the line. A cawing cloud of gulls picked the fresh bluffs of dump.

Blue bet Murphy a ten that he could split the girl's expression open. He slopped over when she finally came and offered a brew and cast his best lines upon the waters and got nothing. She minded her business and respired. Finished unloading, her honcho appeared and she said, "Jack, slay this giant for me."

The kid moved in and Rufus threw him onto the heap. The kid got up and *laughed.* Rufus threw him again and the kid got up again. The third time Rufus said, "This is ridiculous." The girl had the solution: she kicked her door open. Rufus' back was in the door's way and the force and leverage of it pitched him in a neat swandive. Her face lit up with delight and Rufus won his ten. She also bequeathed him her middle finger in parting.

After he took off his mudpack and after he had a better load on, Rufus realized he had planned it all that way. The realization led to further celebration, and when they finally got back with the junk the Chinaman was furious and docked them and put them on separate trucks from then on. His mistake.

What is the meaning of dirty teeth? Murphy's gums began to bleed and he saw it as a catch from Bunny Brown. He had incisor visions of her gorging unknown, unspeakable things. He didn't identify them, couldn't: probe and she had a vanishing act. She was chimerical. He didn't get to see where she lived; she let go of the unlisted phone number but not the address. He pilfered her purse in search of it and her license led to row after row of toffee stucco apartments with louvered windows in El Segundo, and she wasn't there. It was a transient land and no one remembered her. The place unsettled him. It had to be well populated yet it looked evacuated, like a nuclear war site. The dryness left a dust that subtracted color saturation. Every object was coated and turning the shade of the stucco. Dennis didn't even know Bunny's age or place of birth—the license said she wasn't yet twenty-one but she wouldn't verify or deny. She mentioned a brother once.

When she came to see him she tossed clothes out of the bulky canvas overnight bag where she kept all. They sprang up about the room like crumpled lily pads. She never picked up, but rose from the sloth as from the half shell. The clothes actually on her were always clean, precise, carefully picked. She wore microscopic skirts though the style was in twilight, certain jeans yes but no slacks. She wore long-sleeve Ts, scoop and square-cut and boat-neck, that put her breasts to good use, and she was proud of her neck, ashamed of her upper arms. Her neck was lush vanilla and clean, without fagoted divides or simpler crepe. She had a flaring line of collarbone: one she had green-sticked as a child (a boy had jumped on her and, young and malleable, the collarbone had bent rather than broken), a thing she didn't hide, and it had healed in high relief. There was a deep, tendony valley below it, the spot where you can stab down straight into the heart. Her single vulnerability.

She kept up a constant study of herself, her face, chest, slight flab, padded hip. Her upper thighs were cellulite grounds. The short bloom that genes and birth control pills afforded her warred with excess adiposity. But she avoided athletics. "I fuck for exercise," she said. Murphy tried to imagine the sight of her running on some field or court, so low to the ground. The image was laughable. She knew what she was doing.

She didn't tan and hid her skin from direct sun. Two big-brimmed straw hats lived in the back window of her car, and looked like odd-shaped fried eggs under glass, and in heat or glare they came out. She took up residence beneath them and in the shade of dark glasses. Her skin was her fundament; to her her boobs were besides. She had had more than a single reason for staying inside in Joshua Tree. The skin had a fine percale texture, not quite smooth. The slight impasto was carnal somehow: she always seemed to be coming out of herself. Close up, the nubble and grain seemed to be her sexual heat and naked self rising through a glaze. It was easy for a man to feel the cause and pursue the effect. An optical illusion. Let a blotch appear and she could rub her face the pink shade of the hash marks she sometimes had from tight underwear before basting it with cream. She didn't talk about her skin care and her gravity about going to seed. They seemed enormous vanities, but she left them when they were treated to her satisfaction like the scatter about her. They were put aside, and joined her dismissive secrecy. It made the acts seem solely physical, quirks of her largely male bent of mind. No visible woman's despair accompanied them. The concentration about herself, though, made Murphy study too, and she became a ripe mystery.

Murphy had a sniff about people, a quick nosiness, and normally a disdain for further detail. He sized them up with speed and some self-interest. Quick contemplations. The opposite of Blue. Rufus had a sense that people were like hourglasses: beyond the initial possibility of surprise was a great conformity, yet further still, there could be the smallest, deepest idiosyncrasies— the methods of masturbation, the things that bring tears, the sorrows of the heart.

Howard Barr moved to the Playboy building and an indictment came down against him and the office disappeared before the next day. He made the papers and professed innocence loudly, then slipped off to Mexico or further south; there was talk of extradition and lawyers jockeyed. On the other hand, Bunny didn't talk about it and found another job without apparent effort. Her new office was also the art director's dream: mahogany paneling, deep shag, the rooms cubicles fitting into a cube. The name on the door, Ramses Products, told Murphy nothing when he picked her up. She had her own room and he gathered she was well paid and did something invaluable, but what?

He tried to pick an advantageous time to eke information. He thought to try as she rode him: "I wonder why we do the things we do."

"Must you talk?"

He said, "Hazard life and limb, court danger, pestilence, ignorance—"

"Do we care?"

"Well—"

"I sense the beginnings of a prepared text."

"All right then" (subtle, he thought). "How about some facts and figures on old Bunny Brown?"

"They're in your hands, you measure them."

"Just the facts, ma'am." But that did have part of his attention. "Uhh . . . thirty-seven." Consideration. "Twenty-three . . ." Consideration . . .

"The way you're working there, it's as if you're pickin the combination of a lock."

"Sounds good."

"Feels good."

"I'm tumblin with the tumblers."

"They're the best you'll ever have."

"Yeah, but what's inside?"

"No mindfucks," she said.

He turned her over. "What the hell? Are you hiding state secrets? Are you Daniel Ellsbergstein in drag?"

"But he blabbed." She made a noise of derision or orgasm.

"Well—"

"Easy, son."

"—fuck you."

"Son."

"Fuck you, fuck you." he said quickly.

"Oh son Dennis shit."

Her mouth always surprised him. He couldn't tame the harshness or the message. She could gross him out.

In a minute she turned him over. "You're losing it."

"You nympho."

Bunny laughed. "I'm just tryin to get some satisfaction."

"You got more than I got."

"Tell me you didn't come."

"I didn't come."

"Well, some earthquake, then. Hmmm. I wonder if they're going to be any aftershocks."

"Stop manhandling me," he said. "None of that until I get some answers."

"I don't know what you mean."

"You're real name is probably Trudy Gefiltefish and you're scared to admit it."

"You knew. All along you knew," she said, still riding, then sang (she liked to sing), " 'Stand up, stand up for Jesus, ye soldiers of the cross.' "

"Sit on my face," Murphy said.

"That's next. But first." She said, "You're coming back.

"What do you know, we seem to be fucking," she said then, and when she had finished and finished him he dumped her off. At this moment her flesh did nothing for him. He lacked the necessary energy, weak from semen defying gravity.

"That's it," he said, when speaking again seemed a real possibility.

"Oh."

"Enough of this shit."

"Oh?"

Challenged, she began to play magic mouth and fingers.

Before long she looked up from her work, the cat's meow; and he cuffed her and her head went swinging but she held on with her hand and he was hurt more than she was.

"Some things just don't work out," Bunny said.

She got up and cleaned herself out and dressed. They didn't talk until then.

"How's Blue?" she asked.

"He's still waiting his turn."

"Well, give me his number."

He took the dare and she took the number.

"You're not serious?"

"There are other worlds to conquer."

Murphy said, "You know he's part black." He wanted to surprise her.

"M-mm. Well, why not. Once you go black you never go back. So I'm told."

"Who told you that?"

"Martin Luther King. A great stickman."

"Cut the crap."

"You wanted to know my secrets. 'I wish I were in the land of cotton, old times there are not forgot—' "

"You cunt."

"Don't take the Lord's name in vain, son."

Murphy, rising: "Maybe I should give Toni a call."

"I don't mind."

"I like tall girls."

"No boobs."

"Nice ass."

"Wrong end, Buster Brown."

"They both work."

"The truth comes out. No wonder you and Ruf-ass get along so well."

Her soft quick sly lip beat him again but her reaction time wasn't fast enough. She was bouncing off the john door and on the floor in a relationship with the Toro. Her neck hurt, her chocolate panties showed ("fudgies" she called them), but she was lucky to be down there. If she had been up, he would have slugged her not simply shoved her. Up there alone he regretted it already. The result of the action had dried the anger beyond itself: "I'm sorry."

"Hey, that hurt. You take life too seriously." Suddenly stern;

surprise had rattled her and stripped the jape from her, a first.

"I do? My wife didn't agree."

"She must have been a prune."

"Not exactly."

Bunny tucked the chocolate out of shot and organized her legs. She threw her things together, checked herself out, nursed her neck. She said, "I don't like being swept off my feet."

She went out the door and Murphy followed, still naked. Morning mist was thinning and bluish like cigarette smoke; the sun was beginning to fluoresce. Her Karmann Ghia was pulled in next to the Open Road and she slipped her canvas duffel through the cracked window. Murphy didn't know where they were:

"What's next?"

"This girl gets in her car and goes."

"Look, we could cut out for Joshua Tree," he said.

"It's going to be too hot."

"There are solutions for that."

"I've got a job, you know."

"Only for a day or two."

"No can do," she said in mimicry. "I'm not going to get fired like Toni."

"When did she get fired?"

"They canned her when she didn't show up and didn't call in again."

"I thought she said she'd never do that again."

"So she did," said Bunny. "She's crying all the way to Acapulco."

"Acapulco? What's there?"

"*Who's* there. She didn't go alone. She's always wanted a pilot but she settled for a co. She isn't real picky, you know. Why do you think she lives in Manhattan? It's a stew zoo. Before pilots, it used to be helicopter guys. For that matter, how do you think she got to be weather girl?"

Bunny said, "I don't want a copilot."

"What do you want?"

She said, "Did you really think you'd get to me in there?"

"You went too far."

"No, before that."

"I wasn't after your life story, just a little meat and potatoes. Why won't you give a little?"

"I gave at the orifice."

"Won't you ever quit?"

"I thought it was pretty good."

"It was, it was." He said, "I'm not after your balls."

"Well, shall I pack yours to go, Denny?"

"Come on. Get serious."

"Get serious," Bunny said. "See. Hear it."

He heard it and shut up. They stood a minute atop Hollywood.

"Okay," she said. "I'll tell you what you want to know. I'll tell you about me. I have no great ambitions. This is what I want: I want sex and no questions, I want a man who's a good provider, I want to be left alone when I want to be left alone. I like fun but I don't like party lines. 'I've gotta be me,' " she sang. "What else? That's all. That's everything. It's as simple as that."

"Okay," he said.

"Really?"

"Sure."

"You can stop asking?"

"Sure."

"You can stop wanting to ask."

"Sure," he said.

"Or," she said. "Let's say I wanted a good fuck right now, could you do it?"

"Give me five minutes," Murphy said.

She laughed. "Listen to the man. You believe in raising the dead?"

"Routine."

"I can see us waiting and waiting and—you getting arrested." She looked at her fat strapped watch, then reached her small first finger to his stubbied penis. "Time's up. Look what you got. Look what you don't got."

"I fell over you, baby."

It didn't come out simply.

"I guess you did," she said, and opened the Ghia door.

Her breasts lurched as she dipped into it: the cant of them at a slightly downward, perfect angle. Her teeth.

"No contest," she said.

The car started with a cheery snort and she put on her sunglasses and backed up. Her manner had faltered when he had thrown her, but she had regained it, become what she was, the sensation she wanted to be, small girl all cunt. She went out the way she came in.

The morning of their last day the horizon was sallow and becoming brown, like burning peaks of a meringue. Straight up seemed untouched, but the burn was climbing the sky. Before noon any sense of distance would be consumed. Lungs tasted it already and had eight thousand gallons to look forward to before dark. The senses began complaints.

Murphy and Blue were waiting to go. The Chinaman's office, a room off the garage, had route maps for the trucks on the wall. They looked like chest x-rays: the patterns of these recent streets fit as simply as graceless ribs. Murphy's and Blue's territories had a mutual sternum and crisscrossing arrows, the Chinaman's search for the shortest route; never satisfied, he always found new ones. He exalted the axioms of American business—efficiency, ingenuity, gadgetry. This morning his air conditioner needled him during line-up. Not yet 5 A.M. and he still wanted it to work. It whinnied, a fair imitation of his trucks' hydraulics, and it wouldn't cower or cave in to his yells. It whinnied on. The Chinaman turned *r*'s to *l*'s but oddly, without equality or prediction and with a backlash, backrash. The name Rufus was a tongue twister for him, ruthless or lupus or in between. He gave it up; just Blue. Dennis was Dentist Mulfi.

"Goddam ail conditional," he said. "Mulfi fix it. You heal."

"There isn't time now," Murphy said. "I'll do it when we get back."

"All light, get going. I want you back befall noon. I don't want any daughtering around all you filed."

The trucks rumbled out but lights halted their first impressive rush. Their progress lazed as they shed off in different directions. One of the last two, Blue inched and revved and pissed on Murphy, the other, at a light and at the next said, "Get yawl ass in geal," and took him again.

"Oh, ho," Murphy said. He rammed the junk through its gears.

Wheezing diesels, the two did a dance up the Pacific Coast Highway. The intersection of their territories was a half-circle, then a light and a long hill. Blue was ahead at the light; Murphy, down-shifting still, ignored the brake. The engine was braking for him and then the rear of Blue's truck helped. The loader on the side yelped. Blue came down out of the cab.

"Hey, man, watcha trying to do ta mah mah-chine?"

"What are you talking about?"

"You hit me, fucker."

"Your imagination."

"Don't hand me no shit. See this. Now back that heap a trash off."

Dennis in first let the clutch out. *Whump, whump, whump.*

"You can't drive, shithead."

"The hell you say. Beat your ass, Fred."

The black stress vanished: "How much?"

"In this thing? What odds you give me?"

"Ilishmen chickenshlit," said Ruthless.

Murphy shot the junk into reverse, then first again. He pulled up flush.

"You're crazy," his shotgunning loader said.

Rufus' face appeared at that man's window; he had to walk

sidewise to fit through the gap. Murphy leaned across the cab. "Race?" he suggested softly.

Rufus grinned. "Name it."

"One week's tote, you overgrown motherfuck." Still soft.

Blue climbed to his cab. "Call it."

"Vamos."

From a bulb the street became a catheter: it shriveled for the length of the long hill. Neither Murphy or Blue gave way to it. The hoggery insured synchrony. Abreast, they occupied all of it. Lead was a matter of gear shifts, a cab or a quarter length, then correction, and they had to visit sidewalks—there was No Parking but also noncompliance. They had to flow against it, the opposite way, one half of one up on the sidewalk and listing. Once there were cars on both sides: the loaders shinnied and the two trucks made contact, kissing in collision, and then blew through. Chrome tore and hooped, silver snakes wriggling in the air. Side bumpers franked the parked cars, leaving cancellation marks with metallic shrieks, a descant to the larger racket. Bones shook. Hard hats flew. The trucks blasted on undaunted.

They forgot the cans of trash; some they sent spinning and spilling. Pedals were to the floor for openers. Pick up was left for the return, and at the top of the hill they parted.

Beyond the first charge engine grind smoothed. The drivers stopped taking it out on the parts. They flew fluidly street to street. The bet became beside the point: speed hooked them: all they wanted was acceleration and all motion was input: a leap from the bumper, the swing of an individual can, the crank and whimsy of the hydraulics. Well done was also; shoddy was brakes, waste. Such lumbering brutes under such sweet control. The purposeless splendor of it unleashed enormous energy and they planed in the high of it for its own sake.

The trash cans on Blue's side of the street were empty when

Murphy got back to the hill. Blue wasn't in sight. The development reestablished the race. Murphy let it out down the hill. Updraft suctioned light discard from the junk. Mostly white paper, it wheeled and drifted behind like a line of parachutes.

On the Pacific Coast Highway, Murphy found himself screaming but the sound was lost in full bore. On Sepulveda he ignored lights, his left hand standing on the horn. He also ignored the toll at the bottom of the Landfill. He aimed to one side and kept on going.

Beyond it and around the first of the turns he sighted Blue. There were trucks between them, ascending also. They blocked Murphy and were going too slow. Murphy pulled out; again he hit the horn. Blue heard the warning and heeded it and swung out also, but he lacked momentum; he had had to slow to take a place in line. Murphy was just down-shifting into fifth. By a third turn and entry into first he was on Blue's tail. But there was no way around. The right lane emptied and Murphy tried it. Blue just blocked him. Good timing: descending trucks whushed by. The displaced air in their wake jarred them.

The dirt road straightened and widened on the last of the virgin ground and turned down toward the fill. From the virgin plateau they could see it. Here there was room to pull out and Murphy did. The road ahead was empty. Abreast again, they went down with a roar.

What was the finish line? They didn't know and couldn't stop to decide: at full speed they plowed into the piles and garbage exploded. Blue shot in windshield deep. The junk's bin popped free and ricocheted overhead in a slow roll. Its engine choked and died. Gulls scattered like splash.

They were still laughing when two GMC 2500s appeared and barricaded the way behind them. Men fanned out. One in khakis, a thermal T and sunglasses approached. He had Roi Tans in a breast pocket, a red windburn on his cheeks; a Motorola in his GMC crackled. The birds had resettled, so had the trash. The trucks waded in the avalanche. The man with the Roi Tans looked at the scene and chewed his cud a minute. Then he said, *"What the fuck's going on?"*

The orange Cats on the line kept turning it under.

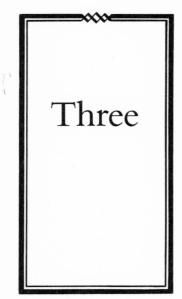

Three

The Raincheck Room was in the limbo of Santa Monica Boulevard. The street there had no hours, it never shut down—the Mayfair was open twenty-four hours, so was Book Circus, the massage parlors 10 A.M. to 4 A.M., Hollyway Cleaners 7 A.M. to 9 P.M. with one-day service, and the Gary or Paris theaters open often by noon. To its north side were stucco and wood frame houses aging promiscuously, sadly. The lingering lay behind jungling landscaping, birds of paradise and wild palms: they leafed out the bright light and razing evidence, the quick changes. Deluxe apartments took their places, better-income property with built-ins as advertised: pools, saunas, frplcs, dns, bm clings, eltric eye pk grgs. They went up with the speed of undercranked film, instant apts; and they ran down as quickly as the stuccos and wood frames they had replaced, nearly as quickly as their occupancy turned over. The depreciation was just another write-off and the residents knew their scene and soon had newer places to go, other deluxes leapfrogging up. To the south, though, there were lawns within a block or two, and ball in the streets. A family community had dug in. They were slowly losing their neighborhood, a grudging attrition that galvanized the remaining spirits. They sank themselves into their bits of land, fixing and fortifying, finding some happiness while under siege.

Santa Monica Boulevard had these, and there were always bodies and enterprise passing through. Every sort. Fliers for them papered the telephone poles and were ripped to snow-flakes and replaced. The flakes fell and blew; the staples and tacks that stuck them nicked the wood and lasted longer. They piled up, a metal lattice like characters of a slapdash language. The poles were double-high and crackled with electric load; you could hear them from the street. There were stains and blots on the walks—some dried and disappeared, others never did. The long-lasting seemed to come out at night, feral tattoos in the sodium light. The artificial glare gave shapes a menace and a verisimilitude: any conjecture upon their sources was possible, and new ones came quickly regardless of day or night. Things happened here.

◆   ◆   ◆

The Raincheck itself was a deep creosote shade but had a red door and no windows. The street penetrated anyway. The twin hums of a Fedders and traffic offered a sort of stereo. At two Happy Hour began and Murphy and Blue were there.

"Just put it on his," Murphy said to Eli, behind the bar.

"Look Mufty it was no contest."

"—I won," Murphy said.

"Forget it."

"None of your shit, Blue."

"This pains me. The wager is insignificant next to the principle involved. I will pick up my own, but can you not admit defeat?"

Rufus never sat at bars. He made no use of the new metal-legged brass-studded stools. He would stand at the trough, leaning on one forearm or the other, his rear end sticking out. The angle brought him down to size until he stood again.

"Over the years," he said, "lo these many, you have never admitted it yet."

Eli laid down another Coors.

"His tab," Blue said.

Eli grunted and put it so. He limped, a very wide, very slow-moving man who could move very quickly. He wore Ts (today a Miller High Life one) to showcase his huge pecs. Back down the bar.

"Like my father," Blue said. "A betting man and welsher. He always bet my mother and never paid off. Check that. I guess he did. He'd beat her up. She used to call herself Black Ann Blue."

Murphy knew he was being placed in shady company. "Well, that's what you got to worry about, me beating you up."

Blue looked over his glass; inscrutable.

"Double or nothing on the darts," said Murphy.

"Farts on the darts."

"I'll give you a handicap."

"Jesus, you're a wriggler."

"Afraid to admit I'll win, huh?"

"All right, you mo'folk." Blue laughed.

Clara stopped on her way by with her tray and dish and change. She wore a short-brimmed pleated denim cap. She was big and had big low unfettered boobs. An alligator on her short-sleeve shirt was trying to scale one of them. "What's funny, Blue?"

"Clara, what isn't?"

"I'm with you, Blue."

"Clara, Clara, Clara."

"What is it, Blue?"

They had an adopted affected contagious way of talking.

"Many things, Clara. For one, Murphy here won't admit he's a motherfolk."

"Ah, yes, I see."

"Tell him he is."

"Murphy, you are."

"Clara?"

"Yes, Murphy."

"You know what Blue is."

"Yes. Of course."

"Tell him."

"You are," Clara said to Blue.

"What? I wasn't listening."

"You are some motherfolk." Clara liked Blue.

"Tell him he lost," said Murphy.

"You lost," Clara said.

"Only a motherfolk would tell me that."

"Yes."

"Tell her who told me she's a motherfolk."

"I am, she is, you are."

Blue switched forearms. "Clara, I am going to have to tell you. I'm no longer among the employed."

"Again," said Clara, as he would.

"Murphy did it. He wouldn't fix my air conditioner."

"Mean," said Clara.

"The man wouldn't fix my air conditioner. I had to fire him. And my air conditioner fired me."

"Listen," Murphy said. "The fucking derby was your fucking idea."

"What's he talking about?" Blue asked Clara.

"I haven't the foggiest."

"Me either. How's tricks?"

A woman appeared and circled, looking for someone? The

baby spot in the dart room backlit her and put her into eclipse (with corona) until she passed to the bar. Her halter dress exposed a skinny back, the vertebrae in relief like a baby about to teethe. She wore sunglasses and many rings. An actress perhaps; Nicholson, Kellerman, Warren Oates—actors hung here. The glass behind the bar was taped with three-by-five cards, movie trivia quizzes; they were spaced about the sectioned edges like patchwork piano keys. The girl dragged a cigarette, kept to herself as Murphy watched.

The sight of her lifted his spirits again. He thought of trying his hand, but she had a forbidding repose. Clara had abandoned Blue to fill orders. Murphy and Blue resumed, talking in low voices, still arguing, sweet nonsense. There can be a beauty to it between friends. They traded friendly obscenity, gave lip. Beer didn't seem to quench the thirst they had; they kept downing more. They found themselves contemplating their life situation, a serious enterprise. Usually they weighed fantastic futurities, but the subject kept threatening to turn unpleasant. For example, they didn't have twenty-six weeks of unemployment checks to look forward to. The California Board of Human Resources wasn't going to be interested in their welfare. Consequences. They returned to lighter matter.

Another man arrived, letting in heat and light and some horrid air. He had a tan that paled his eyes and wore boots, a saddlebag over his shoulder. He set up next to Rufus.

"Hey, how you doing?" he said. "It's bad out there. I was drinking apple juice in my office. The real thick kind. No preservatives. The sky out my window was the same shade. I closed the curtains and turned up the air conditioning and I made a few calls and made a little money and then got out of there. I got this far on my way to the beach. A little reinforcing shot and I'm on my way again. I don't really go in for drinking very much.

I used to, but it's all calories and no content. Do you know Adelle Davis?"

"Haven't had the pleasure," said Rufus.

"She'll tell you. I had dinner with her not too long ago and cornered her. What a woman. Dynamite. She's got to be seventy and looks like fifty. I'm Peter Bodine," the man said, and held out a hand.

He had learned how to not button buttons, a Hollywood strategy. At the throat three were open and the flaps of his pink oxford shirt waffled as he shook hands. His chest disappeared briefly, along with the fair hair there. He had a head of it as well and the right-length muttonchops just filling in, but bad bones. There were odd sharps and flats about his face; it was dented like a poked side of cheese.

Rufus accepted the hand. "Rufus Blue."

"Look at the size of you. Hey, the name sounds familiar. Have I met you? What do you do?"

"I've done many things." Blue was about halfway into the bag.

"That sounds . . . baroque. Let me hear some more."

"Let you hear some more. What would you like?"

"Surprise me," said Peter Bodine.

"Surprise you," Rufus said. "I was a trombone player."

"Any good? I could get you some bookings."

"No longer," said Blue. "Was. Once. At fourteen. When I was eleven I was part of a church group, we called ourselves the Rhythm Aces. We were bad. I was big for my age, had long arms. I picked up an old horn and blew. The slide had rigor mortis but I didn't know. I used my lips until I knew better and got some oil. I wasn't the first to do that. Jack Teagarden did. He got all these liquid qualities barely moving it. Stomach tones. He used his chops. You know trombones? There're seven regular positions." Still leaning, he let his arm play out. It found invisible stations and then went on and found others. "The air column changes the pitch. Sweet notes, though not a sax. I liked the tenor sax but there was this horn in the church cellar. My mother sang there on Sundays and I went with her to rehearsals. Anything to get out of the house. The next year I was going to Lincoln High. The place was a great music factory. This was in Kansas City. I didn't make it very far in school, I lit out. At fourteen I tagged on to Lloyd Hunter's Serenaders. They were big time, almost, but the war had begun and Kansas City had gone dark. Bands took to the road. These men could play and they could talk. I heard about Snub Mosely, Dickie Wells, Sox Maupin, the best trombone men. Moline, Joline, Cairo, like corn syrup, Muscatine and Emporia, Wichita, Sedalia, Carthage, Joplin, *Helena Ark*ansas. Even Oklahoma and I-O-wa. I can hear the conductor calling— my first trip we went by train. After that we went in an old Ford school bus Lloyd had that couldn't hold us. We were stacked under baggage and instruments. Who cared? I didn't. The Serenaders would play anywhere, barns, cornfields, Fairyland Park. It didn't matter. We battled some bands. I was a sideman, a fill-in, a bodyguard, maintenance man, driver, the kid. I hit the centers of notes. If you can lay it down you hit the odd parts and disappear into them. And many of them could. They swung. Many riffs. All they cared about were their pieces and that night's lady. No-good motherfuckers and the best men going."

". . . What happened?"

"My country called me and I went. I became a gunner who never gunned. I got as far as Long Beach and saw the ocean which I wanted to see and I'm still here. The band didn't make it through the war. Some died, some didn't and passed through here one time or another, the old Cotton Club, studio gigs. Lloyd's still here somewhere. He runs a bar or's a mortician. I don't know."

"You don't play anymore either?"

"Other things came along."

"Did you become a beach person? That's where my head's at. In a couple of hours I'll be out there and be able to regain my sanity. First thing tomorrow I'll get up and jog a couple of miles along the beach before breakfast and get it together. Then I'll be ready to come back in and face this madness."

"Actually, I became a stuntman," Rufus said.

"You're kidding. I've played polo with some of you wild men. I've spent time with Yak and Joe Canutt. Dick Kratz was a close friend. Did you know him?"

"I knew the man," Rufus said.

"He was like what you were talking about. What a mother-fucker he was," Bodine said. "A great guy, right?"

"A great guy."

"We used to have a drink or two."

"Kratz didn't drink a drink or two."

"You know what I mean."

"I know what you mean."

"I set him up for a job or two. That's not to mention his wife. Whatever happened to her, I'd like to know?"

"Did you know her?"

"I'd like to have known her a lot better."

"Which wife are we talking about?" said Rufus.

"You mean there was more than one?"

"There was more than one."

"The dynamite brunette. You know, she always had a gorgeous tan."

"You mean Liz, E-liz-a-beth."

"Of course. That's the one."

"She killed herself."

"You're kidding. After he died?"

"Before."

"I didn't know that. Why?"

Rufus said, "How well did you know him again?"

"Oh, you know, I'd see him here and there and we'd hoist a few."

Blue looked at him. "Where was this?"

"All the places. We weren't exactly"—Bodine crossed fore and second fingers—"like this. We didn't socialize in the same circles, but we liked and respected each other."

"A great guy, right?"

"Right."

"Your ass is up to your elbows in pig shit," Rufus said.

"What did you say?"

"Clara."

"Speak to me," Clara said.

"Move Pee Bodine down the line."

"Eli," Clara said.

But Peter Bodine had already backpedaled quickly several feet. There might have been more, but a girl came out of the pinball room.

"I'm sick of pinball," she said. "I'm sick of darts. I'm sick of pool."

The girl wore Indian silver and turquoise rings and bracelets and patched jeans. She had her hair curly and pulled back off her face to further thin her ascetic lines.

To Blue: "Want to see my calluses?"

"I do," he said.

She held her small hands up, palms out and fingers spread, as if saying "Ten," thumbs touching. The central well of each was yellow and hard.

"The machines can't have a chance."

"Well, how come they just wasted me. Tell me that."

"I'm amazed," he said. "Let me stand you one."

"Do me a Dos X," the girl said to Eli.

"I have others to show as well," she said.

"Proceed," Rufus said.

She stepped back and lifted a leg and set it beside his elbow, as to a ballet bar. She was limber and barefoot. Little struggles for purchase and she hiked her jeans to the knee. Just below the caps she had surfer knobs.

"They used to be bigger, like walnuts, walnuts, you know, still in the shell. They were the texture of warts. My board and I had a perfect relationship."

Rufus inspected them. The girl had given up shaving her legs.

"You should have seen them before." she said. "What happened was I got sick of waiting for the perfect wave. Now I'm sick of sittin on my ass."

"Calluses there?" Rufus inquired.

"I feel like I'm dying and I'm sick of dying."

"What else are you sick of?" Rufus asked.

"What I am is sick of the fuckin possibilities," she said. "Do you want to do some dope?"

"Thanks. Some other time."

"Drop some, a little," she said.

"I'll think I'll pass."

"What does that mean?"

"It means—"

"I got some chaparral. It'll clean you out after, so you won't fuck up and get really twisted. Chap's really good for that, you know that? You ever done some tabs? Some tabs would be good."

"How about another Dos?" Rufus offered. He himself was onto Bacardi.

The girl accepted the fresh bottle and took it by the throat and upended it. She drank with greed and abstraction, and a little head dribbled.

"It's the shits," she said finally, after stopping, after saying nothing awhile; she floated away and came back, as moody, as fractious.

"What is that?"

"You go ahead and name it."

She went ahead herself and started to, the sins of the world swallowed and regurgitated whole.

Rufus interrupted: "How's your leg holding up?"

"Oh, that," the girl said. "Leg, how the fuck are you? Leg doesn't answer. Leg's asleep. *Shhh.*"

"Well, Gams," Rufus said. "Maybe we could negotiate the thing to the floor without waking it."

"It sleepwalks."

"Ah," he said. "I should have known."

"You know, I could have them both up there without shit for trouble."

"I'd like to see that."

"Shittin me?"

"God, not I."

"Okay, asshole," she said, and shoved her Dos Equis away.

She set both her hands on the bar a foot in and leaned forward, slowly taking her weight there. She lifted herself onto her hands, her right leg rising. But she didn't stop with legs up. She swung the sleeping left and lifted her right hand, slid the right leg under, then the hand down and the left up and the leg further and under, quickly, both hands down, and she snapped reversed herself. She sat facing him; let her legs dangle.

Her motion was rapid, a little rough, and lovely. It didn't break down into pieces.

"That was beautiful," Rufus said. "You know it."

"You think so?"

"Truly."

"Oh fuck," she said. "The things I used to be able to do."

"Murphy used to do such things."

"Who?"

"Next to me."

"Hey," the girl said. "What can you do? Let's see."

"What?"

"Duty calls," said Blue.

So Murphy put a shot down and using rail and seat as steps stood on the bar. He raised his arms in front of himself as a sleepwalker might, and set—nothing happened a moment: the bar was still and limpid and below him, all its scenes stopped—and did a front flip. The arms in full swing slapped the tucked feet, the shitkickers. Eli had to send out an arm to preserve his shaky landing, and steadied, he immediately did a sharp tight second. A good one, a fine feeling.

For a moment after there was a hush equal to the moment before. Even the forbidding, teething beauty down the bar looked up at him. Rapt, vulnerable, perhaps lonely, probably not twenty-one—from where he was now she seemed nothing of what he had already decided she was; when you're young enough an initial aloofness can be protective cover.

Murphy was still a little out of his own skin. Through himself he could feel the effort of sudden activity, already the reliving of it, and, so quickly done, the linger still of anticipation and preparation. His muscles were animating, the way a dancer's define themselves and cumulate.

He jumped down and retook his place; and bar life resumed.

"He used to do it on barstools or down steps. Back ones," Blue said.

The limber girl nodded and looked down the line to Murphy. "I could take you," she said. "I'll take you in darts. I'll take you in pinball. I'll take you in pool. Name it. Any of you."

Her words were more indictment than challenge. The grace of her stunt had salved her, but Murphy's had brought her down again.

"There's no dispute there," Rufus said.

"What?" she said angrily.

"We believe you," he said softly.

"Don't feed me shit."

"God, not I," he said.

The limber girl laughed and the laughter pierced her acidic, willed bitterness and showed braces, a band and some hardware molar-to-molar along messed upper teeth.

"You can do me," she said then.

"Thank you very much."

"Your turn, Blue," said Clara.

The limber girl waited on him.

He said finally, "I wasn't quite prepared for that."

"Well, what the fuck did you think was going down?"

"Good point," he said.

She had an afterthought, an added incentive: "I give great head."

"Wait a minute," Dennis said, his returned reverie—somersault elated—turning to inspiration. Lightbulbs popped: "Oh, forget Tupperware, forget booze. We are going to develop—" He stopped, tucked tense in. "I am here to announce the development of the shaped fiberglass coffin. The beauty—now listen to this—the beauty of this development is its *unique* double function. It's of course a resting place, streamlined comfortable enduring water-resistant, reasonable in price, available in sizes shapes colors; sequined, even, if you wish; *and* has a removable tongue-shaped lid for preeternity surfing. Care to invest?"

"What's he talking about?" the limber girl asked.

"What he's always talking about," Blue said, "the geetus, the green, the folding, the flip-out."

"Blue, a few shares?"

"Just put it on my tote. Your tote."

"This is no chickenfeed operation under consideration. Put it up motherfo' or lose it. This is the one that's going to do it."

"You're sure?"

"There's no doubt about it."

"Well, there's a slight drawback."

"Yeah?"

♩ "I got me no beans."

The music effected a double bar.

"I can dig it," a man said, one of a threesome. They had come in some time before. "That coffin thing. I've got ideas like that in the works. Bill, this buddy of mine, builds these discount places. He's got like fifteen of them going up and I'm finishing them off for him. I just did one and he likes the work I do. Now, this guy knows what he's doing. He drives *a car,* and carries a roll you wouldn't believe. He says to me whattaya need and I tell him and he rolls it out. Nickel ante to him. Of course, I add on some bucks. He's hip—it's okay with him, it's not hurtin him any. I'm just about to get my contractor's license, and as soon as I do I'm gonna be doing them from the ground up. Anytime now. Do you want to see the schematics? I carry them with me because I like to think about them. Hold on, they're in my truck."

He was out the blazing door, then back unraveling the sheets on the bar. He smoothed the thick paper; its creases crackled. Fingers had worked it before. The few untouched spots were like small ponds. The lines beneath the handling lacked definition, a smudging of reprint and fade. He studied it, smiling. He had an upturned grin: the wide tails of his mouth shot up in sudden parentheses. They didn't open and the closed corners never kept quite still.

The sight to him was proof and explanation enough of what he had said. Then an end let go and the plan rolled and snapped back up. He stuck a crooked forefinger into the side hole and twirled it tight and bapped it against the bar. He had beaten fingers and wide-placed thumbs.

"We could do this with those coffin things of yours. You and me, make a pile, whattaya say, pal." He slapped Dennis on the back, a promissory note. A wink. "You be the idea man and I'll get us off the ground. I've got connections. I've got ideas of my own, too. I've got an offer now," he said, "to run some plants. Be the foreman. I just about have the job. They want me. All I have to do is go down there and take it, and it's good money. I don't know if I want it. I don't like people bossing me."

"Maybe it won't happen," Clara said.

"I know, but you can't be sure. Maybe I should take it. I've got another thing going—" He talked quickly, loudly, leaned his face in as he did, like a co-conspirator; he knew that trick. He had one wily brow and plump folds beneath each eye, a maggot of flesh: a squeeze like recent stupor can leave, or dissolution's lineaments. He jittered limbs and expressions; his motor ran fast.

"—A studio wants me. I've built sets for them and they want to get me into the union. I missed a couple of days, didn't feel like working, and the head man said it didn't matter. 'Take a day off now and then,' he said. 'I covered for you. As long as you work when you're here.' I picked him out right away and stayed close to him. When he was working, so was I. He saw my hammer fly. I know what I'm doing. You get your union papers and you make four or five bills a week. For starters. Then one Thursday they told me they were layin me off as of the next day. I picked up my check and never looked back. What do they think I am? Nobody treats me like that. I get people who do. They could just eat the Friday they had coming.

"I've better things cookin," he said. "This buddy of mine's about to put together this movie with Goldie Hawn. He's real tight with her husband, some foreigner. It's going to be about the service, a documentary like—were you in the service? He wants me to play a part. I was ready to give him ten character ideas right then but I wasn't interested in any minor role. I was in for eight and a half years and did a couple of tours in Nam, but I got out. I saw what was going on. I've got stories to tell." He leaned in again. "I know what's with this country, Kiss-ass-what's-his-name. The Jews are going to take over unless we do something about it. Nixon's just another one. My buddy understood.

"I've been wondering where I was going." he said. "It's all been comin together. Maybe this is it. Movies. I can see myself in movies. Just let me in the door. If I can get to talk to a producer —just get into his office and I'm in. That's my trip."

He turned to the girl with him, smiled again. She had a dark exotic closed face.

"My old lady's already done some work for TV. They're always after her. They see she's got something. She did some dancing for a big show, one of those pilots, with the guy who played the doctor—What's his name? The fugitive. They really liked her."

"Some how I find all this hard to believe," Rufus said.

"It's going to happen. I'm going to send her to one of those acting schools, that one they're always talking about on Hollywood Boulevard. What's the name of it? She's going to go places. Aren't you, hon?"

She didn't say a word. She chewed gum, her midriff bare, a

chiquita perhaps. They peppered the county, alighting and then quickly, suddenly looking Californian. They tossed away their apparent underpinnings and grasped American flash and tack. Little Jesuses, statuettes and prints, were chucked to the rear of closets behind the silver platform shoes. They turned sunny side up but opaque; the transformation wasn't all it seemed. The paraphernalia was a substitution more than a change. Madonnas and prostitutes—underneath, the myths they brought and retained were often sharply Mexican.

The third of them next to her was leathery and older and working shot glasses. He was sunburned, and rolled balls of peel between his fingers, then dropped them into an ashtray and lit them.

The three of them together were without common heritage or haberdasher; they had no congruity.

The talker lit a Benson and Hedges menthol and tapped his pockets and his glossy white patent leather shoes. "I've got some pictures of her." He dug out a packet of color slides and dealt the first to Murphy. With cardboard rims, they looked like 3-D lenses. It propellered in. "Here, take a look."

The slide and girl and dress were all dark. Dennis aimed it at the dart-room spot. Squint. The light opened it up to detail: she was tied to a chair in it, squirming.

"She got paid for doing it. I went over and watched and took the shot. A hundred and a quarter for an hour and a half. Not bad. Better than where she works regular. She works one of those spots near the airport in Inglewood or somewhere, and she's got to take it off and walk around and serve those flyboys. I'm going to change that, aren't I, honey?"

"*Ya no me quiero que dar mas aqui. No mas es pura habla.*" Her swift slurred Latin-Spanish was as quick a chatter as an electric typewriter.

The talker smiled. The third man peeled. Murphy passed the slide down.

And Leroy came in.

"Who wants to go a few rounds? Blue, you mother?"

"Yo."

"You just missed a show. Clara!" He greeted her, and Murphy, and stepped to the rail and into the journey of the slide. "What's this, travel pix?"

"Have a look," the talker said.

"Look at the little witch. Who is she?"

"Right down here. Whattaya think?"

Leroy double-taked: she looked dour roped in, not exciting. On the barstool in the middle of a smoky Raincheck afternoon she looked gaudy and shy.

"Hey, hey, baby, I'll set you free."

"She's my old lady," the talker said. "I hitched up with her so she could stay in the country. I'm teaching her about things."

"I can see that," Leroy said. "Showing her the ropes."

"She's going to be an actress. I'm going to send her to that place on Hollywood Boulevard. You know the one."

"The Actors Studio," said Clara. "Isn't that hard to get into?"

"I'll swing it. They may want me, too."

"A lot of sweet pieces can't cut it on film," said Leroy.

"Why, Leroy," Clara said. "Tell us about it."

"Well, they can't. Their expressions close and harden, their eyes midget, their pores open up into acne piles. It's strange stuff."

"That's it," the talker said. "That's what I mean." He went back to his slides; wrong ones riffled by his search like stacking poker chips. He tried a couple to the light, found one: "See."

Leroy lined it up. "Sweet Jeez-uzz. I take it all back."

"Pretty good, huh."

Leroy looked again, and reluctantly passed it. Dennis' turn: in this one she leaned against a railing against a bright dark sky. No clothes. Light poured through her centerfolded skin. She was backlit and frontlit, all breast and bush. She wasn't a *chiquita* any longer.

"She's little, there's nothing there. I should know. I have trouble . . . getting it on with her, if you must know." He smiled again. "But in these things she's all over the place. She's got it on film. She blows up."

The slide returned and Leroy ogled again the area of profound transparency.

Curiosity sidled Peter Bodine back up the bar. He'd been trying to move in unsuccessfully on the girl ten feet down. He waited for the slide to come his way.

"They're others here, plenty more where that came from," the talker said, noticing him. He slid his top chip along the bar, past arms and glasses, to Bodine. "I shot them on my porch one Sunday morning. You should have seen the neighbors."

Bodine took a long look and then walked it back personally. He stuck out his hand and his shirt waffled. "My name's Peter Bodine and I run an agency here in town and I think I might be able to do something with these if you're interested. This town's always honking for new talent. Bob Evans is looking for a new face, I was just talking to him. He isn't the only one. How many more of these shots do you have?"

The talker thumbed his stack.

"Is she . . . mixin it up in any?"

"What do you have in mind?" All cage.

Bodine took a look at the subject matter of their discussion. "Is she interested in that? Only for starters, of course. I think an audience could off on her. She looks to me as if she's got what it takes."

"What are we talking?"

"With one call we might get something moving. I know the people who are just getting a picture off the ground. The financing's there. It's going to be an X, but with a big budget, and funky. They're searching for a face and . . . she'd do nicely for the part."

"How big?"

"This is the sequel and there's the girl from the original, but your girl'd have the chance for the real activity. She'd have the shot to steal the show. I think she could very well do it, too. They'd want some stills, sure, and a test or two. That's why I asked about others you might have."

"I got some I can show you." He shuffled: "How's this?"

Bodine looked. "Very nice, now we're talking."

He passed it along: here, still alone, she held a fluorescent tube; her legs were parted and the tube poised. Just beyond the shutter click was a possible stunt.

The talker said, "I'd want to be in on the action."

"I can't say, but I'm sure you could if things worked out."

"What are we talking about? What kind of bread?"

"I heard you before talking hundreds. Think thousands." Bodine added, "That is, under the right conditions."

"Under the right conditions she'd ball a fire hydrant."

"They might have a bit more in mind than that."

"Under the right conditions."

The talker smiled.

Rufus had been silent a long time. He said now, "Put your picture postcards away, pimp, and move on down the line."

Negotiations suddenly fell through.

"What'd you say, buddy?"

"Just move along."

"I'm conducting business. Don't interfere when I'm doing business."

"I don't like your business."

"Nobody tells me about my business."

"Just move along," Rufus said again.

"Don't fool with me. If we weren't drinking together, and if I didn't kind of like you, I could destroy you. I wasn't in the service for nothing. They taught me ways and I learned ways."

"Do your style," said Leroy.

"I could take you, too, as well as the big motherfucker."

"The last you said"—Blue's voice grew even softer—"don't do it again."

The peeler stopped peeling.

"Nobody interrupts me when I'm doin business and tells me what to do, *motherfucker*. I heard them call you that. *Mother-fucker.*

"They can do what they want," Rufus said.

"I do what I want. *Mother-fuck-er.*"

"All right," Rufus said.

The peeler spoke then. "I smell a yellow rose, a yellow Ne-grose."

Rufus looked over; he looked sleepy. Murphy's glass set itself down. Leroy cleared himself from the bar. People checked out their space. The stillness came alive and dangerous.

"Shit," the limber girl said. "Not another duke-out."

"You sick of them?" Rufus said after a minute.

"God, am I ever sick of them," she said. "What a bore."

"I'll go a few rounds with *you*," said Leroy.

"You couldn't beat my meat," the limber girl said.

Leroy recovered quickly. "But, baby, I could swim your quim."

"Go stroke your joke."

Leroy laughed. "Where are they coming from? They just don't make these bags like they used to."

"Poor Leroy."

"Comfort me, Clara." He hugged her and, with his height, found himself staring eye to eye at the scaling alligator.

"Can I at least have the other one," he said to it.

"Well, fuck this shit," the limber girl said from her left field. She got down from the bar and, limping slightly, her leg still sleepy, she walked toward the pinball room.

Before she reached it the talker moved behind Rufus and picked up the stool Rufus didn't use and swung it. The sick thud it made upon contact put Blue down and launched Dennis. Before he knew it he was up on the bar on his right arm, slamming the talker with his bad left. He wanted the man's smile. Everything in him wanted to end it. A little high, he lost his balance and the follow-through floored him.

Falling, Murphy saw Bodine kick Blue and saw Clara moving. He saw her legs to the knee and then to the crotch; her pants snugged into a woman's hollow there. He saw Bodine levitate, his boots lift and show their soles, his saddlebags separating wings. He saw Blue. The sights were sharp and splintered and virtually disconnected. Somewhere down the bar there was other action.

Before Murphy got to his knees the *chiquita* laid the limber girl's bottle of Dos Equis over his head. He got up anyway and shed her. She tried to hold on and left tracks with her nails and mouth. Where was Leroy? The peeler gurgled between Eli's bicep and forearm. People seemed missing. Murphy started to turn to look, and sight on one side faded out. He was hit. His attempt at orientation had been a mistake. The time it took he didn't have. There were more blows.

This time he floated down and saw nothing special. He crawled into a lot of wooden legs. Stools. They were inanimate and friendly, a place to hide. Acquaintanceship was short—they were movable and they went. The ouches from their pokes as they evacuated began neural paroxysms. Pain. Against the bar he stood somehow. He was still taking it. A shriek came out, pure rage. He punched the motherfucker out.

Four

Light skewered space: the sky was blinding and seemed to be falling. It was hard and hot and waxy, like looking into a new car hood. Faces in it turned to carrion and others pickled behind tinted glass.

Inside the sheriff's car there were no armrests and no inside door handles in the back seat. Murphy tried to lift an arm: it retained flexion but chafed and stuck. The skin wanted to stay with the seatcovers. No a/c either. The hands also resisted because they were in handcuffs. Murphy jockeyed a shoulder after some sweat running down from his hair toward his eye. His shirt caught it and came back red. The sweat was blood. The discovery brought wonder, then claustrophobia.

Next to him Leroy said, "Let me out of these things, will ya. I didn't do anything."

"Can't do it," one of the two cops in front said.

"You sons of bitches," Leroy said.

"You gotta be crazy to be a cop," the one who was driving and had spoken said. "Have all these suckers call you like that. They are beating their brains out and you try and stop them and they take it out on you for trying to. You're trying to keep them from hurting themselves. I've seen it hundreds of times and I laugh at em. You hit em? No, laugh at em. That drives em out of their gourd."

The one listening had just begun a mustache.

"Of course, there's another breed you can't fool around with. That sucker Devlin and Petty took. The one the barman had under his arm. Don't fool with that. Keep your eye on the quiet ones, and if you see anything out of the ordinary at all, even if you only smell something, you get your piece out front and arm's length, as big as you can get it in front of him, and use it if you want to and have to and ask questions later. The same goes with a knife, I don't care if it's a pinsticker or a Gerber Magnum. Don't mess with them, loonies like them, and don't let them hypnotize you either. Well, look what we got behind us. See—on the bike, he's a dick."

He nodded at the rear-view mirror and the second one looked back. There was a long-haired man behind them on a low-slung chopper with high sweeping handlebars. His mustache had handlebars, too.

"I hate cops," Leroy said.

"What are you complaining about, you derelict?"

"What'd I do to rate this?"

"What'd *you* do? I suppose you're right. You weren't doing much when we arrived, unlike your buddy here. He wasn't foolin around."

"I got blind-sided."

"You should pick on people your own size."

"I hate cops."

"We got that."

"What happened?"

"That's going to be our question and you better have some answers. You got any priors?"

"I don't understand it," Leroy said. "Goddam, I just walk peaceably into a bar, and of all the ones in all the world, I had to show up in this one. How did I get into this? This isn't a fate I deserve. I'm a good guy, aren't I, Murphy?" He adjusted his body several times unsuccessfully: comfort wasn't to be had. "At least you could put some armrests in this boat."

"Dry it up, dipshit."

Murphy meanwhile was trying to hold himself down. Careful thought, he thought, and things would straighten out. The mention of his name elicited motor responses. Dizzy, he leaned forward and tried to mutter. He wanted the window opened. The word wouldn't get out. Other things were there, and lunch came up. He blew it forward through the wire divider.

"Goddam it," the cop driving said. "Goddam it to hell. That's going to cost you, sucker."

While he was in jail Murphy had two visitors.
First Clara:

"How're things, Murphy?"

"Less than great, Clara."

"What are you doing here?"

"I don't know, but here I am."

"But why you?"

"They seemed to think I know what happened."

"I told them what happened," Clara said. "They asked and asked me and I told and told them."

"They don't believe that I don't, really."

"Has a doctor seen you?"

"I got a cold shower, some new clothes." He plucked at his shirt: he wore issue and an I.D. bracelet.

"You don't look . . . fabulous."

"I had the runs for a while. Which made me very popular."

"They could set your nose at least."

He was aware it had been moved but hadn't seen it. He said, "Can I be a star now, finally?"

"Just as soon as they remove the *s* turn from it."

"Just what I always wanted."

"It doesn't matter, Murphy." She said, "I could just kiss you."

"Well, just tool on over here."

"I'd do it."

Picture a tongue rolling and wadding to get tippytip through:

there was wire between them. He imagined it, but she didn't try. The crosshatch broke up her face and put her a distance away. There wasn't glass at least. She wore pants—he had never seen her in anything else—but she was hatless, unlike at work, and her hair was down and long. It aproned her face and chest until, sitting down, she tossed it back. A bruise curved along a cheekbone, a discolored boomerang. She looked big and blooming and he felt a heavy sensory response. His jointed horns sure, but something more. He wasn't sure quite what: its cut was as deep as adolescent pain.

She said, "You were wonderful."

"I really don't—*really*—remember."

"How could you? You were too busy."

"Rufus and I came in for a drink. A fight started and I got knocked out. Something like that."

"No wonder they don't believe you. That's not what happened at all. You guys were already celebrating when I came on. I don't know what. Blue said you had left work early: the air conditioner had breathed fire or something. Which doesn't make sense, but the day was noxious. You had a serious discussion about the tab, whose it was, and when I stopped by you were calling each other the usual names, and while you were at it Blue managed to get a free hand onto my ass."

"See. I don't remember that."

"Nicely," Clara said.

"It's a nice ass."

"I work hard enough on it."

"Ummmm," Murphy said.

"It was a very heavy afternoon, a weird collection. You guys kept getting into discussions with them. Blue told one Joe Hollywood he was full of it. The guy wanted to make a scene but took a look at Blue and withered. Sally was there in a bad way and

a drunk in a booth who kept calling me over, and he had a bad
case of filthy-mouth disease. And some guy with pictures of his
Chicano wife. He was hustling her. He was really hustling himself, and every time I came back to the bar he had switched pipe
dreams. He kept jumping around and his mouth twitched. I kept
expecting him to lay his dirty hands on me, thinking he was
probably a sneaky feeler. I was ready to fend him off but he never
looked my way. Glad for it, but I would like to have let him
have it if he tried. He just kept on talking. You had done one
of your numbers on the bar and Sally was sitting on the bar. She
got down and started to go and the first thing I saw was you
hitting the guy. But you went down and he didn't and his little
puta hit you with a bottle."

"What happened to her?"

Clara smiled. "I took care of her."

"I'll bet you did."

"The guy kept hitting you and you went down, three times
I think, but you were never out. You'd go down and you'd get
up and go down again. Then you got up and went berserk. It
was so beautiful. You just destroyed him. Eli finally had to pull
you off, and he sat you down and told me to call the cops and
to serve you one on the house. I did and you sat and drank it.
You were never out."

"What else happened?"

"Well, everybody else was. Leroy took it from the silent guy
with the mustache. Eli threw Joe Hollywood into the dart room.
Eli was pretty beautiful, too. Then he took care of the guy with
the mustache."

"But Blue," Murphy said.

"He's in the hospital."

Murphy almost knew: "Bad?"

"Lucky Blue. The doctors say his skull should be scrambled

eggs. He shouldn't be alive. I guess he's so thick-headed it doesn't matter what you hit him with. His head's all wrapped up in this huge turban. He's all right but he hates the hospital and won't talk to anyone. I go before work and he nods at me, I know he knows me, but he isn't talking. I never saw the guy hit him, only you must have, Murphy, and he would have hit Blue again. Killed him. Lucky Blue."

There was retention there: Blue going down. So large a frame makes a scary flop as dead meat. But Murphy hadn't seen the blow. It was the concussive impact he had reacted to, and he still heard it: it was in his head to stay and to listen to, a permanent loop. The rest of noise had become a packing of quiet about it. Beyond it his memory had no linear track, all action and adaptability syndrome. But the guy had had to come between Murphy and Blue to pick up the stool, Murphy knew, and he knew he should have seen it coming.

Clara said, "Not so the girl at the end of the bar."

"Who?"

"The one who was smoking and by herself."

"The skinny beauty. I remember her."

"The knife the guy with the mustache pulled and threw at you hit her and she died the next day."

"I didn't know," Murphy said, and despite her cheering and thanking attempt, they ran out of things to say.

The second to come was Paul:

"Well, you finally made it, Dad."

The opening pained Murphy: he didn't want more visitors, and not his son to see him here.

"Kidding, Dad," his son said, when he said nothing. "You okay?"

"How'd you find out I was here?"

"Mom heard."

"She knows?"

"Yeah. I guess they try and call a relative, and they thought she was one. You must carry her name on you somewhere."

"What did she say?"

"She told me you were here and I said I'd come down."

"She didn't say anything about coming herself?"

"She said something about not coming."

Dennis said, "She say anything else?"

Paul let his shoulders rise and fall. "Not much. You know Mom." And he dismissed the matter.

The importance of what she said or didn't say wasn't so much to him. He had a casualness and a languid confidence, a Valley child. The dry sun baked excess and some interest away; people there matured early and had an enormous capacity for disinterest and survival. His tight skin and hair were a buff-brown, sand flats at low tide. Pat's. His height was his own and multiple vitamins. He wore Hang-Ten sneaks and wheat jeans, a western shirt with snaps not buttons. Long hair, some serious acne on the fade. Each time his father saw him he was changed.

"I said I'd come down and see about bail."

"I don't want you to do that."

"Doesn't matter. They said out there it wasn't necessary anyway. They're going to release you on your own recognizance, or something. One cop said you were just being held for the time being."

"I'm sorry you have to come, Pablo."

"I didn't have to."

"Anyway."

Murphy had more to say but it escaped the shapes of words.

"I didn't mind. I'd never been in a jail before. I wanted to see what one's like."

"Great," his father said.

"What'd you do, Dad?"

"Not enough," Murphy said, and after a minute: "I was in a fight."

"I'd hate to see the other guy."

Murphy waited another minute and changed the subject: "You look pretty good, Champ."

"I'm okay."

"You getting some exercise?"

"Been playing a little tennis," Paul said. "Yeah." And he began a shortened, imagined forehand. The scything forearm bulged and veins raveled, bluish twine; the game put bulk there atop its inherited size. At the wrist the arm was rubbed red.

"What happened to the swimming?"

"I gave that up years ago, Dad. Too much work. You have to get up too early, and all that chlorine."

"You were pretty good, weren't you?"

"Naa, not really. I'm better at tennis."

"Tennis?" The game lay outside Murphy's provinces and imaginings; it went, he thought, with another way of life. "Who do you play with?"

"There was a team at school," Paul said. "Harold plays."

"You whip his ass?"

"Not when I started out. He's not so bad."

Dennis stepped on his feelings. He said, "Is that the reason for your wrist the way it is?"

"Oh, that. Weejee gave me an Indian suntan."

"A what?"

"An Indian suntan. You know"—Paul set his hands next to each other fisted lightly and twisted them in opposite directions, as if squeezing out wet laundry—" you do that to somebody's wrist. Weejee's just discovered it and she's been practicing on me." Weejee was his stepsister.

"You see her pretty often?"

"She's been living with us."

Murphy hadn't known. "How's your friend Jeannie?"

"Who?"

"You know."

"Oh," his son said. "She's long gone."

"I thought that was serious."

The shoulders moved. "We broke up."

With license and woman just won, Paul had swung into the Nichols Canyon lot, his swaggery braking lifting dust plumes. Jeannie with him: she was little and shapely and cynical and proud to be the first holding down the shotgun seat. The first in the bucket, and her dusky orange Afro jiggled in the canyon wind, gentle oscillations. Her hair could have been sets of tiny springs. Murphy, home for once, in good shape for once, came out. Here was the mysterious father eying her. Eying him: she looked from one to the other of the two men. She didn't see much similarity. Paul was full of oats. He had only the temporary piece of paper with the state seal on it so far; the permanent calling card took thirty to forty-five days. ***DO NOT LAMINATE*** it would say, and the photographs on them were now to be in color. The temporary was good enough, plus woman: and he had the two necessities of sixteen-year-old southland identification. She knew she had won a role, but she didn't realize its subsequent limitations; other new musts would come and supplant that day's. But Murphy remembered her: she was the first girl he had seen with his son.

"Maybe she didn't like it that your hair was so long."

"I don't think that was it, Dad."

"Well, you could use a haircut."

"Thanks, Dad. That's the reason I came down here, to get that piece of advice. I just couldn't decide about the length on my own."

"I'll pay for it."

"Wow. You're not in for bank robbery, are ya?"

"I will."

"What are those things creeping below your ears, Dad? They look a lot like sideburns to me."

"When did you become such a wise guy? You know what happens to wise guys."

"I ought to, you used to tell me often enough." He said, "My whole generation is like this."

"I doubt that. Maybe you ought to buckle down and get a job and stop hacking around."

"Aye, aye." He threw a salute, mocking a gesture that had been an intimacy. Paul had learned early his father had been in the Navy, learned salutes, ranks, ship's names. His first bedroom had had bunk beds and portholes, a stateroom effect. "I'll just follow your example."

"I ought to throw you out the window."

"That's a felony, Dad."

Murphy seethed. "Do you talk like this to your mother?"

"No, I save it for you," Paul said. "I have lots of time to."

"What does that mean?"

"Nothing. Just could you wait until you get out of jail before you begin delivering your lectures."

Murphy thought he'd been a good father a decade, then a good father *in absentia*. Now this load.

Paul backed off a little. "Anyway, I've got a job for the summer delivering for Trader Joe's."

"The booze place?" Murphy asked. "You're not delivering anything besides liquor, are you?"

"What do you mean? This is the one in Sherman Oaks."

"There's more than one?"

"They're a couple of them now."

"Well, watch yourself," his father said. "This is the Valley we're talking about." He said, "What are you doing with the money they pay you?"

"Spending it."

"Stupid question," Murphy said.

"Not all of it. I bought a car with some, a '55 Mercedes with a sun roof, and seats that adjust all the way back." He threw back his father's look: they had their uses.

"Does the thing run?"

"Just barely. It gets to the drive-in. The rest I'm saving." Paul said, "What I'd like to have is a Porsche 911 with a rack on the back. They really move out."

"That'll set you back a few thou. You have that kind of money?"

"Well," Paul said, "I might have been able to swing one for graduation. Harold said I could have a car of my choice. I'm not sure he exactly had a 911 in mind but I was sure tempted to find out."

"Good old Harold."

"I didn't do it, Dad."

"I guess he does all right."

"He's been playing the stock market. He has me looking out for new chains—hamburgers, sporting goods, House of Pies. When I spot one he checks it out. Beer 'n' Brew, Steak and Ale, something like that—that's what he's talking about now. There's stock coming out. *Float* it. That's what they call it, he explained it to me. Do you know what a dollar in McDonald's in 1957 is worth now?"

Murphy said, "Probably Trader Joe's is next."

"Hey, that's not bad. I'll tell him. He's also going to buy a boat when we move to Laguna."

"When you what?"

"October first."

"I didn't know," Murphy said. "It's definite? It's all right with you?"

"With college I won't be around much by then." Paul said, "There are a lot of good courts down there."

Murphy said, "What does your mother think about it?"

"She's all for it."

"Oh," Dennis said; and then he asked, "Is she still trying to drag you guys along to the snappery?"

"That battle was over long ago, Dad."

"You mean she actually gave up?"

"She never gives up. We just never go and she never says anything about it anymore."

"That's the babe. *That* sounds like she hasn't changed."

The shoulders again: "She's different since she was sick."

"Sick, she's never sick."

"This spring she was. She thought it was just the flu and kept on going, but it turned out to be walking pneumonia. Nobody knows how she got it. The quake did flip her out a bit. Pat was on his way to early-morning practice when it happened and he didn't bother to call. He just went ahead and swam."

"How is he?"

"He's okay I guess. Who knows?" Paul said. "But it was a couple of months after that. She was really wiped out. She'd feel better and try and get up and keep relapsing. In the morning she'd be okay, but by afternoon she'd have a fever of a hundred and three. The thing wouldn't go away. She didn't have the strength to go up and down stairs for over a month. She had no energy at all. She couldn't do anything. When she was finally getting better she still had to rest halfway up flights. It was like walking with somebody having an asthma attack. She lost twenty-five pounds. She's okay, but I think it's one reason we're moving. Harold's doing it because of her."

"I didn't know." Murphy said, and he felt the words over and over.

He'd deluded himself about his way of life. He'd lived to not miss anything, but he'd lived as he'd made it through the fight —with spectacular tunnel vision. He'd missed a skinny girl dying and the daily stuff: his sons' and wife's lives, their raw trivia and real truth.

"I'm gonna clean up my act," he said to his son.

"Sure, Dad," his son said.

Rufus Blue sat up and tapped his head: what a way to bring a family together. He had a child on his lap. The kid tried to stand and scale the knees and thighs. His feet were strategic weapons. Gail was out to here and now Gar's present woman already possessed this climber. She was twenty-three, divorced, looked athletic, a tight Coppertone ad. But was she rich? Another foot landed. Rufus reached out and swiped legs from under him. The kid landed on his rear end away from the groin back toward the knees and laughed. So did Blue. He was good with children; on a limited basis free spirits are. The child was also therapy for him.

Here with him were Gar, Gail, and Janie full of rage; she looked like her grandmother. Chris, his fourth child, was somewhere near Hue. He had had the four in just over five years and the rapidity hadn't helped the marriage, his first.

Janie said, "Are you going to talk today, Father?"

"Here, I'll take him, Mr. Blue. Come on, Josh," his mother, Pamela, said.

"Noo. Wanta stay here," Josh said.

"Come on. That's a big fella." She took him against her chest and shoulders. Josh grunted as Blue had and pinched her shirt between thumb and fingers and held on.

To Gail, Pamela said, "What do you hope it's going to be?"

"Oh, we don't care. Whatever comes out will be all right. We're using Lamaze, did you? I've been practicing my breathing."

She blew air out of her mouth explosively. Her hair was long and straight and she blossomed in a full-length batik dress. Frank, the other half of her we, hung back near the wall silently; he was skinny except for wild fronds of hair.

Gar carried his hands in jean pockets and wore a polo shirt, like Clara had at the Raincheck.

"No, I was a chicken and went under. But I lost fifteen pounds in the first week and had no trouble getting back on my feet. I even rode two weeks later. That was a bit of an error."

"That's bravery," Gail said.

"Insanity," said Gar.

"You should talk," Pamela said. "It's probably too late now, but what you might have tried is trampolining. Someone told me if you do it right it's really good for the thigh muscles. I never quite believed it, though."

"You know, I never believed people when all they did was talk about their kids," Gail said. "It was all so boring. Now look it."

"I know it," Pamela said. "You are going to breast-feed."

"Oh yeah."

"Get the right bra, one that's really comfortable. You don't wear them, well, boy will they be sensitive. And you're carrying an especially lot around."

"You're embarrassing the men in the room," Janie said.

"It's good for them," Pamela said. "A little shoptalk from the real world."

"That's not the real world," Janie said.

Pamela produced an Adolfo bag. "I brought a couple of things you might be able to use."

Gar poured himself a glass of water from the pitcher on the table, then stuck the flowers Gail had brought into it. His father watched.

"Doing another Eastwood," Gar said to him. "I'll be up in San Francisco off and on for a month on it. Could be all right. Don Siegel."

The director's name wasn't only information, it was also evidence of Gar's expectation.

Blue nodded.

Janie said, "Will you come and see me?"

"Just give me your demonstration schedule and the address of the jail."

"Funny."

Blue spoke. "What's this?"

"Nothing," Janie said.

"Janie spends most of her time getting arrested these days."

"What for?"

"See," Janie said. "He doesn't even know what's going on."

"What's going on?"

"Our imperialistic government is killing innocent people. And the Governor of New York stands by while unarmed prisoners get slaughtered and blames the deaths of the guards on them when it was the pigs who in fact slaughtered them."

"Ah," said Blue. "I see."

"What are you doing about it?"

"What am I supposed to be doing?"

"All concerned people must take whatever action is necessary to stop the way we're going. You wouldn't know, you've never done anything for anybody in your life."

"Lay off, Janie," Gar said.

"He's always just *fucked* around. He's never done a thing for any of us, has he? Name one. And now we're supposed to show up and be sweet and cluck over him." She spat the words. "Just look around at what's in this hospital. Vietnam."

"Did you come just to see that and confirm your own set of beliefs?" Frank said.

A nurse came in. "All right, who owns the Great Dane?"

"Do you mean Rex?" Pamela said.

"I don't know his name, but he's big and black and he's loose."

"But how'd he get loose?"

"I don't know, but he's roaming the halls. Rather, he's patrolling them and everyone's running for cover."

"You mean he's inside?"

The door opened partway; a big black head appeared.

"He sure is," the nurse said.

"Rex," Pamela said.

"Rex!" Josh said.

Rufus tapped his head, tapped out the new dimensions of his helmet. This was the third, smaller at least. Away at the inside of the cocoon was a head.

His head still hurt. Tap tap. Tap tap tap.

The human brain is an irregular globe of moist, jellylike tissue that weighs about three pounds and contains more than ten billion nerve cells. It still keeps its secrets and the doctors hadn't been exactly sure what to do with Blue. After the emergency ward and immediate treatment he'd been moved to Wadsworth, a veterans' hospital, and was lucky to get in. He had been hit in the head in the Navy, but "non-service connected"; he wasn't sixty-five and Vietnam vets were filling the beds.

He lay awake with some pain. He was familiar with pain but not the disorientation he also felt. There was a distance between the world and where he was and he was having trouble coming back. He lay and looked out the window at the sick, the lame, the lazy; in administration that was how veterans there were informally classified. The V.A. had a lot of land around Sawtelle Boulevard where Wadsworth was, a complex as large as a college campus. The buildings were W.P.A.; each day the window painted the same primitive—out-of-time streets and shade trees, doctors actually in white coats, a pendulous old man holding his head in his hands at the bus stop, another old man shanking polyfoam golf balls, and a spastic in black-and-white sneakers carrying a rake. Blue could see, too, the domiciliary and the men who came to the prosthetics ward. These were the ambulatory, the ones in remission, amputated a.k. and b.k., above knee and below knee. Sometimes they'd leave with more limbs than they'd arrived with.

The doctors tried to get Blue up. He didn't feel like it, the muzziness, and motor-control difficulties. They considered Brentwood, the neuropsychiatric center catty-corner, and then transferred him to Long Beach. More tests. This wasn't a campus; it was a vast winged building, general medical and surgical and a spinal-cord center. Listless Blue. But in Long Beach they didn't stand for that. These people had religion—the struggle between good works and hopelessness—and he was putty in their hands. Gretchen, his therapist, had him in and out of Hubbard tanks twice a day and she worked him over on a flat board. The water and her hands dug after twinges and muscle atrophy. They couldn't find nerve damage, but it could baffle diagnosis. The slightest whiplash could injure and no tests find harm, no treatment heal; and when it was found, it couldn't be set like a limb. Besides Blue, there were over a hundred and fifty paraplegics, and some quadriplegics. Gretchen, his Führer, stopped bed care and feeding. She said, "You can get up if you want to. Some can't. Why should I be doing it for you?"

So he had to fend for himself, get up and walk. The hospital had no steps but emergency ones and long corridors. He wasn't alone in the hallways in his pin-stripe bathrobe, and the doors were open and he could see in other rooms. They could be rough sights. In them were those with things missing or broken who couldn't recover and didn't die. Some were the wounded you never see, who never knew what hit them and had never known anything since, however long. They had no company but bladder bags and the peanut-butter-size Vaseline jars. They barely added shape to the sheets. Tax dollars kept them alive. Some others had just arrived. They were young and wasted, and at night Rufus could hear one scream down the hall. In his sleep the boy couldn't stop and in the day he didn't remember and never screamed. He never complained. He was Chris's age.

A stool on the head and Blue could hardly walk. He was, as far as they could find out, physiologically okay, but there were many others learning to live with wheels. They knew too well where they were and their eyes pitted from the effort of doing things never again simply done, a tiredness that never went away. They had the levelest gazes; they looked at the world the way others didn't, a combat stare. Antagonism, inquisition, why? And, finally, in their eyes was the drop by drop acceptance of pain, how then the simplest sights became new.

Rufus walked the crowded halls past the crowded rooms. Gretchen would walk partway with him. She was a tall girl, with rough, dry, tight skin and grey eyes and hair the shade of driftwood. He still moved cautiously.

"What do you think?" she asked. "A nasty crack, some lost weight, some unsteadiness. The double vision's gone."

"Yes."

"There're no other residual effects."

"A headache."

"That should go away in time."

"You keep telling me that."

"I kept telling you you could walk, too."

"You call this walking."

"You're moving one foot in front of the other, aren't you?"

"Sort of."

"Well, you're very lucky."

The sun lay in the corridor that connected the old section of the building to the new, and jellied the wax floor. The wheelchairs seemed to roll on water. The motorized whined. The ocean was in the hot still air, as it had been twenty-five years before when Blue had been in this town, a normal Long Beach afternoon. The old ceilings were still being lowered and there was support work under way in the wake of the Sylmar quake.

Thirty-three veterans had died there, the floors of the hospital collapsing one upon another like concrete flapjacks.

"It's crowded these days, except for the help we need," Gretchen said. "From Sylmar, but they were mostly geriatric, the ones who survived. But we're beginning to get the World War Two men now. They're getting on. And from Nam," she said. "Still from Nam."

The hall around them was busy with hurting, getting on, surviving life. The life reached Blue. Gretchen stuck her hands in her uniform pants: it pulled her trousers across her ass, and she shifted her weight and a buttock rose and a buttock fell. Life there, too, and Blue felt well enough to reach out and touch it.

Tap tap. Tap tap tap.

A set of legs and some driftwood hair, and Blue's cock throbbed like a bruise. Now if only his head would stop. He had to relearn the equivalent of walking inside there, too. Thoughts would bubble up and then slide away like mercury; he couldn't hold on to them. His memory failed him. He'd get hold of a piece, tweeze it into place like a shaky surgeon, and then lose it. They just disappeared, chunks of his life snatched away in a series of kidnappings. It was not having the choice that made him care. He brooded, he probed, he concentrated. Still they got away. The defeats tired and angered Blue, and made him feel fragile, a new thing for him. He felt as if he were losing his mind.

Start with simple things, he decided, what he could still work up: a set of legs and some driftwood hair. Sights. Physical things. Murphy, for example, he remembered, had a breast fixation—do you know how many names there are for breasts? So many so funny, Blue'd lose his subject. Call them stuff. Murphy would be appalled. In states of intoxication or wonder Dennis carried on about such stuff. Size and consistency. Odes to aureoles. Legs were more to Blue's liking, that wishbony line.

Enlarge the subject cautiously. Women. Blue was an unusual member of his species. His machismo centered on women, not on competition with other men. The ones that had been in his life weren't a tally or notches on his belt. He didn't blow up with braggadocio, he didn't rate and measure them, he didn't break them down, he didn't get nostalgic. Each woman was a separate glass of water. Rufus took them as they came and gave them room. The generosity was also a selfishness; it gave him room back—unless one crowded, and then she was gone.

Carefully, he thought about them, and the musician in him set to work: could the key to all be the way hips move while making love? Diagram the arcs and curves in three-dimensional space, find correspondence to notes on a scale, and set the motion to music. This would not appall Murphy. Wait a minute, here, he would say. Forget Rorschach. Compose pullulation.

Tap tap. Pullulate: was that what it meant? He couldn't recall. Was there anybody at home? Blue's command of words came from paperbacks, like *30 Days to an Astounding Vocabulary*. He bought them all and finished none, and only odd lots stuck. He had that sort of intelligence: ignorance barnacled by knowledge. He knew how to carve a saxophone reed out of whalebone, he knew how to tie any knot, he knew what the sun could do to skin. He studied the properties of melanin. The auspices for this knowledge was survival at sea: Blue wanted to sail around the world, and he learned about ham radios, the life span of canned goods, navigation and tides, the sun and the weather. His study of skin, though, was also one into his own degree of darkness.

For years he messed with boats. There was never the money for anything satisfactory; the largest he ever owned was a twenty-six-footer. Its tenure was brief and after it was gone he tried racing smaller classes. His size and weight overwhelmed them and made tacking ridiculous; no matter how deftly he moved, comparatively, he lumbered. He got down finally to sailing dinghies. In them, no one could really move, so it didn't matter. They were fun and brutal. The best raced in the East in the winter. That wasn't for Blue, and he tried another alternative, speed. He made a deal on a second-hand Boston whaler and heaved a third-hand Mercury onto its transom. With clamps and a hollow aluminum tube, he fitted a length of broomstick to the outboard's grip handle. Ignoring any other steering then, he stood where a mast might and the boat leveled as it planed. Worth an extra knot. Blue liked that tall, speeding image of himself. The actual doing it soon bored him, but his sons loved the boat. Did they come to see him or it? He knew the temporary answer at least, and gave the boat to Gar. Blue believed the person who wanted a thing most had a right to it.

After the whaler was gone he took to rowing his dinghy. Chris still came to see him and he would sit in the stern and try to trim the ship to his father's satisfaction. He never could. The wriggling attempts only made him more unsuccessful and his rear end more sore; the nylon lining of his bathing suit made lithographs on him there and his father's legs and feet hemmed him in. Why didn't the oars smash the kneecaps? Chris knew they had to, yet they never did. The patellas always found a place to go. He didn't understand it.

Rufus knew none of that, but he did know Chris watched the whirlpools made by each stroke of the oars. Blue did too: the eddies spun and danced away from the blades, as gay and individual as snowflakes. They inspired reverie, and then sorrow as they began to wobble, but with Blue's long, strong, languid strokes, the next began its own twisting dervish before the first could die, and the next, and they kept beginning and falling away to starboard and port, disappearing before they could so each had no end.

The way Rufus let things happen, the way he knew they would, included fatherhood. He wasn't conventionally tutorial. His discipline was unilateral but intermittent; it included work but not play. Work required repetition, as simple or as sedulous as necessary. The dip and the bend of his body while rowing, his back laying in and his legs laying out, his wrist's rolling over and snapping powerfully, were highly practiced. There were hours behind such things, thought and purpose, hard work. He expected the same of others. Afterwards was another story. He could lie around with the best. Literally. There he would be on the floor, like Gulliver, as small live things, his children, crawled all over him and crashed into furniture or hung dangerously over stairwells. Possible catastrophe didn't disturb his beatitude. He didn't bother to move or wake, and they didn't tumble over. Sometimes he'd even join the rug rats, crash around and hang with them. His children otherwise had the normal number of mishaps and injuries, a development in itself that placed his original marriage in jeopardy.

Unlike Connie, his first wife Jan was a stern tight-assed woman who loved him dutifully and hated him pleasurably. Their marriage was a passionate mistake. They waged war, dug in strategically for sieges, and called angry, yet libidinous, truces. Sex, even later on, after a seismic session with their lawyers, had been wonderful and wanton, but had little to do with keeping them together, and it didn't.

Jan believed in charities, the best schools, proper dress, and she worked hard to save her children from Blue. After the divorce she shut him out of her existence—she never saw him again. She climbed socially, and took to buying only American things, big cars, better home appliances. She wore snail earrings and certain-height heels, she grew even more taut and trim. She remarried and moved to Pasadena, and each time after the maid cleaned the house she re-vacuumed it. She could never keep quite still. The happiness she built was tied as tight as piano wire.

And her attempted instillation of values ricocheted. Gar inherited her social grace but used it to smooth over his following in his father's footsteps. His training was more civilized, his discipline greater, his techniques more contemporary, but the stunts he lived for were of greater and greater danger and audacity. He outdid his father, he bettered Rufus' feats. Gail had been a good girl, the perfect child, until she ran off with Frank. Her mother so disapproved she couldn't see the adjective still applied and that others were being added one by one—strong, clear, certain. Janie inherited her mother's name and stubbornness, and inverted her social consciousness. When she was young she was gay as well as willful and, if she cared, a perfectionist. She took then to cutting her father's hair. He put himself in her hands, but wasn't a guinea pig long. Soon he was an artisan's subject. She bought scissors and kept them sharp and shined. She soaked brushes clean. She tested shampoos. He would lie back as she worked his hair and close his eyes, profoundly relax. But woe to him who fell asleep.

Her rebellion came like her sudden anger, without seeming warning, and she attacked her parents, blaming them equally: her bigotry, his chauvinism, her stuffiness, his absence. She found soapboxes and developed a sharp tongue. She pursued wickedness with a fervor. She would show them, stun them—and they kept refusing to be horrified to her satisfaction.

Chris had that capability and he managed it without radicalism. He wasn't a talker, yet he had a quiet knack: when he did speak he could pierce things others wanted and were afraid of, things they believed were secret. It wasn't telepathic, but like an invasion of the knottiest privacies. People around him often felt unprotected.

Chris shared his father's skin and wanted to know about it. Blue's heritage was a subject he assiduously avoided. The first times he successfully dismissed it. Every week, though, Chris would ask when he came and his quizzing wore his father down, and became the only child to hear about his grandparents. The boy soaked up the stories as they worked together sandpapering the boat, a rapt audience. The quiet avidity allowed his father to let go, retouch his childhood. One Sunday when he finally ran down, Rufus watched his son continue to work. He plucked him up then, as lightly as if the boy were a lamp or a ball, tucked him under one arm. He strode down to the sea and tossed Chris in. It wasn't a dunk or a drop. It was a put. The boy soared, and just before splashdown, he smiled.

Jan had wanted Chris to go to college and she had taken to wearing an American-flag pin, a sign of a newly developed patriotism. Then Chris enlisted in the Marines. She didn't want *him* to have to fight. She was ready to go to any lengths to stop it and he wouldn't let her. For as long as he was in she wouldn't be able to settle the disparity this unveiled inside herself. She felt naked in a way she had vowed to never feel again.

Even Blue, who knew the Navy and had no romantic notions about patriotism, was affected. His time in the service had been a disaster shared, yet he had a feeling for it practically as deep as love, and as untalked about. This had elements of farce: the rotten food, the dirty toilets, the nasty homosexuals, the silly rules and regulations, all but death, enjoyed great verbal mockery. Black humor and blacker boasting were how he dealt with trouble and pain, and a part of him wished his sons knew all this, were part of the experience. Now Chris had it, and Vietnam.

Such thoughts visited Blue during his last days at Long Beach. Often, too, then he refereed paraplegic basketball games. The men in chairs found an outlet in them and began to play regularly. The air crackled with their effort and enjoyment, their energy and noise; some of them were amazingly dexterous, surprisingly graceful; none gave any quarter. The games were savage and resurrective. The chairs were bound up with one another and, even set apart by an able body, a zebra-striped shirt and a head bandage, so in some way was Blue. He loved the games, and he was the only one they let officiate. And once, as he blew a whistle and called a foul, he turned and there was Janie watching. Her eyes had the same blaze as the players did, and, as if their ransom had been paid, the kidnapped pieces of his life returned:

There was Junie Huemmer with the most perfect behind he'd ever seen, and there was Connie's red pigment and wheat-germ freckles and gelid-looking throat, <u>all of her</u>, and the way ninety-seven bananas looked at C.C. Brown's stacked against the wall, and the way they looked and smelled when they came up after eating all ninety-seven of them, and the smell of brine near the sea and the smell of sawdust, and Chris sandpapering, his hands, the way they looked, and the way they looked and felt ten years later, as he shipped out, and Gar's first bike ride, and a ribbon in Gail's hair that matched the one in his stepdaughter Nancy's hair, and where was Nancy, and the long lustrous length of hair of a girl named Dorie Winner, and how young she had been, and the shapes of it like wind on water, and sitting in the barber's chair he'd bought for Clara, after trying alone to lift it onto his back like a pack, exhausted and defeated, watching the water and such wind, the westering sun whitecapping it, the light like that in Janie's eyes, and Murphy, Dennis Murphy, and a set of legs and some driftwood hair.

They came at him like tracers now. The opposite of before, he couldn't dodge them or slow them down.

In the GMC they sat outside the Saloon at sunset. Blue was out at last, a cause for celebration. They'd driven the San Diego freeway north exit to exit and bar to bar before settling down to pass some time at the Pastime. The Saloon was next, but they waited outside as the light buttered and then grew orange. For a while the muting shades were a visible rain. They lit the air and cab as gels might and the dimming changings had a grounding weight, an eschatology.

"It's a strange, weird place out here all right," Blue said.

"Out here where?"

"Out here in the real world."

"Ready to go back?"

"Ain't no way."

They fell into their shorthand. The blow and jail and hospitals had only shortened it, expanded implicitude. They ruled out many words and subjects, there were things they didn't talk or think about. Women and sport and sex and talltale and nonsense sure, but not their emotions. They lay in the shortest of shorthand, ish kabibble. They occurred and were passed on; they occurred and were. Conscious inductive reasoning went by the boards. Decisions were feelings and snaps, the pop in wrist wrestling. The economy was an ethos their own size: they had knit a common ground from cities escaped, from things burned out, from deep thoughts, and become each other's roots.

Murphy asked Blue, "How do you feel?"

"It's like getting out of the service again," said Blue. "The mind doesn't know what to do with it all." Horns and disk brakes still startled him.

"Welcome home."

"I think I may be ready for the rocking chair."

"Life begins at forty-four," Murphy said.

"Sweet music," said Blue. "The kids came," he said then.

"We'll bury the motherfuckers," Murphy said.

"Did we go through that?" Blue felt his still-bandaged head with his fingers as for braille.

"You mentioned it."

"They came all at once once. Except Chris. I think we lived through it, but they're ready to be rid of the old man."

"Ain't no other way."

Blue said, "You gotta love the trails we leave."

The streetlights fritzed, blinked. They came on and slowly consolidated light, icing the dusk and the cab.

"What about Clara?" Murphy asked "What are you waiting for?"

"Good question."

"Lookin good," Murphy said.

"I know," said Blue.

"Well . . . ?"

"In good time."

"There is no good time," Murphy said. "I'm not going to let you off that easy."

"Murphy."

There was warning in the word, and it closed down Murphy's kidded truth and attempted convincing, Rufus' having to deal with it; it closed down the discussion. They were as close to argument as either wanted to get.

The Saloon suctioned the evening traffic.

"Look at it, Murphy," Blue said then, "all the tits and snatch and ass. Look at it, the sheer numbers. Is it not the greatest, the very greatest you've ever seen?"

"You're well," Murphy laughed. "You're ready."

Women, and men, overwhelmed the dark, so much that Blue's appreciation was also a sort of grief. There were just too many. With dusk in Beverly Hills the luncheon and shopping crowd scattered and the real estate and law offices and post office across the street flushed into the streets and into the Saloon, among other places, and show people, and those who wanted to be, just dressed or redressed arrived for their evening's work. The Saloon offered another kind of employment line.

The women had rubbed their cheeks to heighten them and they wore this year this month this day velvet strands around their necks and high shoes, and tailored name pant suits and many name layers and name slender metal belts and name clutch bags, and they wore backless braless name tops that looked like scarfs and skin-fit name denim and muslin pants, as cane cutters would, and aviator glasses, and got in and out of little or large name cars. Wonderful parts, physical and purchasable. This was a town beside a city where many women wanted to be sex objects: it was their dream and they and their many men fit to the dream. Here were Murphy and Blue, but inside (despite the glorious parts and no underwear *there*) they couldn't make a successful move. They weren't tan, they had no bucks. So they drank, Murphy in nose guard and Blue in turban, and moved on searching for company, and what else?

Maybe they could wait until Chalet Gourmet closed, don waders, unravel fishing lines, oil rods and reels, gain successful entry, and cast into the tanks where live fish indolently swam. Real sport fishing. They contemplated the idea as they sat on a curb above Sunset Boulevard between stops. Maybe they could—

The next possibility was interrupted by a screech and a crunch, a fender bender. Glass tinkled and a single piece of a brake light jigged toward them. The accident was hard to understand. Lawns were clipped, topiary hung in the dark air like shapes of animals out of a fantastic zoo. This was a quiet street. Epithets rose around the collision and one involved walked away from the argument and the scene. Her heels on the street sounded almost like the glass. She had fine lines and lime pants. She walked under a streetlight and Murphy and Blue could see her flesh pale the already pale shade. Maybe they could cast for her, but she moved with such mission they didn't. She kept on.

After a while they got up and made more stops, looking, but it was a failed odyssey, and late and desperate, sodden and losing mood, the two men welcomed two women walking on Holloway Drive.

"You a hockey goalie or something?" one asked Murphy. But they accepted the bandaged novelty. In Sears tops, their bellies exposed, the women wore in turn white jeans, creased and starched like ducks, and dark jeans yoked with a zagging red stitch. Their dress was different from the woman in lime pants, or those in the Saloon, but as staged. Fashion mattered on the market where they were also, the presentation of body and dress like latitude and longitude. They offered theirs and they took as well the measure of many men. Murphy's mask and Blue's helmet were idiosyncrasies, and they knew such specimens could be dropped should better pickings arrive. It was just a night anyway.

One had white hair hived like cotton candy and no breasts, the other had henna hair and big bones packed with flesh. The redhead also had a brutal basso and a singular talent: she could get her mouth around a shot glass, lean down and let her lips slide over it and grip it between her gums and then throw her head back and chug it; then set it down again. She liked to do it. On occasion the suddenly empty glass would suction her tongue and the glass would magnify it; it would wad and worm before coming loose. She proved her talent again and again, and Murphy and Blue followed suit. They all four drank, the flat girl draining a tumbler. After the first drunk, further drinking brought a second ebullience. They were swept up in it, a good loud time, yet none of them stopped checking out other possibilities.

So late and in their shape there was little chance of better alignments, and they stayed together and managed later to jam haphazardly into the GMC. They made it to Blue's house in Venice, a block from the beach. At first Blue had rented it as a garage, and then later, poorer, his third marriage broken up, he'd moved in. The yard became the garage and the inside slowly developed walls and differing ceilings and small rooms. The house divided in odd jobs as he had specific need and saw fit; skeletal joists still stuck out where he hadn't worked. A parachute covered the lack of a living-room ceiling in petal-like folds. The outside hadn't changed either, its red roofing shingle tacked up like real brick.

Once inside there was no kidding around, the girls made no bones.

"I'm ready," the flat one said. "Lead me to it."

She investigated and found no bedroom. "Look, I'm not getting it off in that thing outside," she said. "Besides, it's cold."

"How about some eats. What's on the menu?" the redhead said.

"A jug of wine, a loaf of bread and a cow," Murphy said.

"Har dee har."

She attacked the refrigerator and slapped some lonely pickles around. "This thing's a morgue."

"You're supposed to say 'Moo,' " Murphy said.

"I got it," she said. "Boy, did I get it."

"What is this place anyhow?" the other one said. "What a hole."

"There's no place like home," said Rufus.

To Red: "I told you in the can we should have dumped these jokers."

"You aren't exactly queens yourselves," Murphy said.

Blue pointed to the convertible. "Ladies, I believe I have here what you are looking for."

"Check it out," the redhead said. "Check. It. Out."

The lean machine pulled a cushion and plumped it. She looked around to the other two in the room. "Oh, is this an all-skate?"

"What?"

"Oh. No, huh. Well, okay," Then she said, "On your marks, get set—"

"So how about we take a look-see," the redhead said to Murphy.

So Murphy toured again the galley kitchen, the hall, the toolroom. Across from the toolroom's long workbench and power tools were Quad speakers, like radiators on pedestals. A solid row of LPs ran along the floor between them, the thin edges of many chewed free of I.D. The redhead didn't glance at the surroundings though. She made for the can and jimmied down pants and drawers. She squatted casually on the john, let her intestines rip. Murphy wasn't prepared for such a state of intimacy, and backpedaled. She kept on ripping. When she was done she got up and looked over the contents of the bowl and looked at herself in the mirror. Then she wriggled her pants up over flaring hips and flushed. Murphy was well outside the door.

"That's better," she said. "Hey."

"Hey what?"

"All aboard who's gettin aboard."

"Right."

"I wouldn't say you're speed off the mark."

"I'm just savoring the moment."

"Save the savor. Let's ball."

It was damp on the toolroom floor and there were many smells. Woman now but also wood chips and the must from a throw rug and salt and a wet reek of eucalyptus from the branches at the window. They made sex seem already on the floor before them. The redhead had a wild wet tongue around the mask but a dry hole. She lacked natural juice and the dry made friction and squeak. She jumped to the touch, the way thin wired women do, despite the tire around her. She had copious chest and belly and Murphy lowered his head to them, a delaying action; food for thought. She hadn't bothered to zip up. Her hands grasped his head from her navel well.

"What are you doing? Are you going down on me?"

Mumble mumble.

"What if you're dirty?"

"—*I'm* dirty?"

"You better not be dirty."

He pulled back, Listerine and crabs on the mind. Then he spit into the dry.

She shook.

Through intoxicated torpor came reluctant lust and he managed to get the red stitching off her great rear and they managed to get his knees sore and then her own. Sanitation acknowledged, no holes were barred. Later they joined the other two.

There were bodies to extricate from in the morning after. One was Blue on his back, snoring and erect. His own and a girl's flesh were coupled; it was a lack of space rather than a specific intimacy. Her head was thrown away and her mouth agape and her lips looked chapped, last scabs of a lip gloss like a sugar glaze. She had a foot and some leg under a blanket Blue had fallen out of. She snored lightly, too. There was also a red-head.

Murphy made it to the bathroom past these sights and vomited. Quick up-heaves, then intermittent. The bathroom was tiny and had a skylight, a plastic bubble; with dawn it was the shade of a television screen. In between, when he could, Murphy turned to it and thought, but not deep thought. Bathroom thoughts. Simple profound cliché thoughts and dreams.

He thought about what he'd wanted for himself: a shipshape self and some unspecified, undemanding success. He had always wanted a perfect flight, the perfect fuck: this was how he organized and simplified his categories of thought. They became his test cases. In the air would be the abandon after the fear and then the utter serenity; and afterwards he would meet her and she would say (right away), "I like you." He: "I like you." She: "Let's fuck." It was important that the dialogue play this way, and they would. There would be the abandon and then serenity and perhaps abandon once again. Simple. Virtually it had happened, but it hadn't solved his life, and it hadn't altered or diminished the dream. He remembered a girl, not Pat, not the girl in lime pants (he had already forgotten her), but one he had seen years before in a tomato-shade turtleneck. The tomato tomato. He had only glimpsed her and he had wanted to throw everything else into the wind. Virtually other times he had, but the want didn't stop, and he still remembered the girl in the turtleneck. There was a lech beyond getting his nut, a mystery. It did not end.

The sickness kept coming until thought ceased; even women washed out of his mind. The vomit scrubbed it empty. It wouldn't allow coexistence, and, finally, he only wanted quiet most of all. The sickness felt like it was in his hands and testicles as well as in his intestines. He had always felt a free agent and now he felt carried along, a reluctant passenger. And he was afraid. He was reduced to a child in sin: let it stop, let it stop and I'll be good. Anything You say.

At last he could leave the bathroom. The others were still snoring and he wandered outside. There was a wind and a fine sheen of flying sand. He leaned against the ex-storeroom next to the ex-garage, where Blue had made windows of the walls and set chairs inside. The salt air rinsed his face. He knew his recent vomits weren't simple. His life was coming up.

Murphy stood a long time waiting for strength before Blue came out. Blue managed the porch and the steps all right but tripped over his bike. The frame snared his foot when he wasn't looking. Blue swore at it and shook it off and made it to his feet again carefully. Then he picked the bike up and threw it onto the roof. With its departure a beer keg was left in the sand yard, and a '56 T-bird top.

Blue said, "I never use the thing anyway. How come no one steals it? What do they think I leave it out here for?"

Murphy cleared his throat, an oyster bed. "Could be they don't want it either."

"Why not, it's perfectly good."

"Not now."

"What?"

"They're built to ride, not jump on and throw on top of a house."

"What are you talking about?"

"Nothing important."

"How you feel? I feel good," said Blue. "But you don't look so good."

They shared saffron palettes. Wings of it parted from Murphy's reset nose, the dying bruises from the break; Blue's complete face was sallow.

"It was a long night."

"There's someone alive inside. I woke up next to something that was making noise. Strange-looking thing."

"You're ripped."

"What? I feel good."

"You're still totally ripped." Murphy said, "It's probably your mother."

Blue thought it over. "I don't think so."

"You may be right."

"Connie's in there."

Murphy's turn: "What!?"

"She doesn't look so great either."

"She isn't in there."

"I remember last night," Rufus said. "About time she came back."

Murphy began to wonder about this peculiar Blue. He had nothing on but his turban and the fall had set it loose.

"I always told her to take care of herself. She used to be a luscious fat beauty, remember?" said Blue. "But who's the other one?"

"You're out of it, Blue."

"Couple or three boozes—nothing serious. I feel good."

"Count again."

"Couple or three more than a couple a three, what the hell."

"You're pie-eyed."

Rufus said, "I'm a sober judge."

"You're a low-life motherfucker."

Rufus wasn't impressed. "I've heard it all before. Water off the back."

"You're a low-life motherfucker you are." He felt the quick elation of their camaraderie.

"Fighting words," Blue said.

"Used to be."

Blue considered that: "I could go a few rounds. I feel good."

"You said that before."

To show proof Blue put dukes up experimentally and began to move, to box. The footwork sent up splashes of sand to match his visible breaths, and his turban grew a tail. He was a sight, so lean from lost weight, loose parts jumping up and down.

Murphy had to laugh. "You look great."

"I told you." Blue said. "Remember the welterweight, the one we saw fight in Tijuana with the quick jab and the quick feet. He fought in circles, remember. That was his attitude. Circle to the left and jab, circle and jab, those quick combinations."

"He lost."

"But he was good. Better. The best."

Blue kept on, and as he did, the awkward dance and loose parts gathered languid grace. And the yard could have been a ring: in first light it looked whitewashed and pearly like canvas under floodlamps. He moved by the windowed ex-storeroom across the yard to the GMC. The weathered and bright shacks glided behind him. They were ringside along with Murphy and morning and the cairn of Pacific Ocean Park. They passed and returned and passed again.

"He lost," Murphy said.

"That's not the point," Blue said, but he stopped. His breaths were very audible as well as visible. He had a bridal train now.

"What's the point, then?" asked Murphy.

"The point is he was good and we enjoyed him. I did. He was worth it."

"Murphy," Blue said. "I beat you in that garbage truck. I just remembered. I tore you apart."

"Are you kidding? I won't go for that bait. Not again."

"Only the truth."

Blue came over and also leaned against the ex-storeroom. He said, "You know, I like your nose."

"Fuck you, Blue."

"No, I truly admire it. I think of it often with great fondness. I look at it and it makes me happy. After studying it I am able to go out and enjoy life. Without it—" A last jab: "I often wish I had one like it."

"You asshole," Murphy said softly.

"*Gracias,*" Blue said.

"*De nada,*" Murphy said.

Blue cupped his genitals, still out of breath. "I think I ruined myself."

"There was no point in trying to stop you."

"Of course not," said Blue. "What's this?"

He discovered his shedding head and ran through the loose as through ticker. Then he began to wrap it around his penis, making a sling for it. "I knew I'd find a use for this," he said.

The cold was getting to them and the ex-storeroom was locked and unheated anyway. They looked through the built-up stubble towards the sea. The piece in sight in the offing could have been pebbled slate. The pebbling was movement, the waves coming in, but the sight continued to be the same.

"What's next?" Murphy said.

"Who knows?" Blue said. "Got cold feet and gonna go home and blow the horn awhile."

Polar bears, they went back in.

Blue fell down on the way, listing backwards at first like a runner suffering an oxygen shortage. Murphy gave him a light prod when he didn't get right up.

"Come on, Blue. You'll really freeze your nuts off."

Blue didn't respond; *now* he conked out.

Murphy bent down and his head hurt, hangover's greeting. He could drag Blue by his cold feet to the house steps. From there he had to lift him: which was easier said than done. Even skinnied Blue was two hundred and twenty to two hundred and thirty pounds. The messed bandaging ran around him like swaddling clothes. A light gust lifted sand a foot, playing over both of them. It nipped the flesh like pinpricks. Squatted, Murphy had to squinch his eyes and spit.

He set himself, his hands and forearms under Blue. He was still on his feet but ass down, his knees fully bent like a weightlifter after clean but before jerk. He grunted and got Blue up. The long legs flopped away as he tried to keep track of the head. He couldn't manage to straighten up. Careful steps at a time, jack-knifed, Murphy got him to the door. It presented a problem. He kicked it and it held, he turned and hipped it and it held. He didn't look forward to grappling with Rufus down a second time. The door's old porcelain knob was level with his mouth

but a slippery moon. He went back to an old technique: he butted
the door with his head, and it popped open.

He laid Blue inside by the one heater. Murphy couldn't reach
the parachute and pull it down, so he found and spread a Hud-
son's Bay over him. He found a pair of socks and raised and got
them over the big feet. He was ready to leave him to search the
kitchen for something hot and stomach-settling when the breathing stopped.

Murphy didn't believe it at first. He refused the silence he
heard. The face slowly turned the shade of the sea. The shade was
unmistakably eternity.

It got Murphy onto his knees. He shook the body, struck the
breastbone with a fist. Fingers in the mouth found the tongue
missing. He fished the gullet and brought it up. He hit the breast
again and then tried between the shoulder blades. Reluctantly
Blue gagged and got sick. Murphy cleared it away. The body
didn't do more. He leaned the head back and pulled down the
jaw. He put his mouth over Rufus' and blew.

Murphy lifted his mouth and let go of the nose. He waited
and repeated.

His hands felt the heart beat.

The terrific feeling he got in response to that passed quickly.
This was labor. How long could he keep going, could he stop?
He didn't know. Asinine love prodded him and early malingering
lessons. Certain situations called for certain reactions, Q.E.D.
There weren't choices. There were less and less, though, of these
when he wanted more.

But this one he hadn't wanted—*but* he had it. He had a role
to play, and he felt it launch and lock into place like a passing
gear. He forgot his own concerns, the cold and cramps, his sore
knees and stomach, and then remembered them again. They went
away and came back with greater pain. His same position made

his muscles rage and separate. They declared independence in different kinds and colors of ache, and marked time passing. The wood floor became an aggressor. He had been cold but sweat broke. It ran into the corners of his eyes and wet his shirt. Water poured off of him. He kept going. As close as he could measure he pushed the head back and pinched the nose twelve times a minute and breathed into Blue's mouth.

One of the girls, the titless one, stumbled out of the bathroom. Her hive had fallen and snarled. She shaded her eyes to see. "What's goin on?" she said. "Another sexual?"

Murphy came up.

"What are you doin?"

"Call an ambulance."

"What?" She waited while his head bent in and backed off again.

"Did you hear me?"

"What's goin on?" she said.

"The phone," Murphy said. "Now."

She went for it, moving as if aboard ship. Between breaths Murphy directed her. She was slowly awakening. She found it and was with it a long time. She came back finally. "It doesn't work."

"It doesn't work," he gasped.

"That's what I said. It's dead."

"Go down to the corner. There's a booth there."

She said, "I'm freezing."

"Do it."

"I've got to find my clothes."

"Fuck your clothes."

"I'm not going out without shoes." She went in search of them, a pale shivering sliver. She came back snapping up ducks. Rufus' shirt on, unbuttoned. One shoe.

"I can't find my blouse. I'm not going without the other shoe."

"Yes you are."

"I don't have a dime."

"Turn a trick."

"You're a laugh riot."

"Goodbye," Murphy said. "So long."

"I'm not going without my other shoe."

Murphy said, "If I have to get up from here I'll kill you."

The words were to be believed and orgy haze slid back and she left without the second shoe. But came back. "Where are we? What's the ocean doing out there? Where do I tell them to come?"

He told her.

After she was gone, there was a mouth-to-mouth again. The breathing. Gradually he fell inside the air. In this second wind there were spaces but no elapsed time. The respiration became meditation. He felt in slipstream.

The girl returned and Murphy told her to wait outside. Time then began to stretch. Minutes were like hours. Hope and heroism deserted his actions. So did peace. He struggled out of habit and because there was nothing else to do. The same pace, the same methodical and yet quick pace. He took a breath, he bent, he blew. There were no prayers. There was no fear. He was exhausted and didn't feel it. He was resigned. Breathe, bend, blow. They had no apparent effect. Breathe, bend, blow. He had fragments of sight, the knots on a six-inch swatch of floor, a fingernail, how much nail, how much pink, the dried salt spatter on the window, a grain of sand. Breathe, bend, blow. He felt outside of himself as just before and just after a stunt. His breathing and Blue's silence and his own self became inseparable. Breathe, bend, blow.

So he didn't know the fire department rescue squad came

quickly. The two men wore black pants and white shirts with name tags at the chest pocket. They carried scissors at the belt and had pads in their back pockets like meter maids, and they went to work. They eased Murphy aside.

There was tougher than where he had been before.

"He doesn't look too good," one said. "What happened?"

"He stopped breathing."

The man looked around at the unfinished ceiling, the parachute, the unrolled couch, the occupants. "How did it happen?"

Murphy began with the morning, not the night before. Then he said, "He was just in the hospital."

"What for?"

"A head injury."

"What kind?"

"He was hit there."

"With what?"

"A barstool."

"How long was he in?"

"A couple of weeks."

"What'd they say about it?"

"I don't know," Murphy said.

"What hospital?"

"Long Beach Veterans." And Murphy said, "What is it?"

"Can't be sure, but we're not taking chances."

The other said, "Well, it looks serious, doesn't it?"

He had gotten the gurney and run it in. He collapsed it and the two lifted Blue on; except for the lifting they moved very quickly. The second sprung the stretcher up again and they were on their way. The first worked from beside, got a plastic respirator in. They wasted no time. Rufus' legs hung over the end of the stretcher. Darned socks.

His chest moved: he was breathing alone. His eyes opened when the two men slid him into the rescue squad.

Murphy said his name.

The eyes moved but not the head.

"Blue?"

A shove and the top of him disappeared and then the socks. One of the men broke out the oxygen.

Murphy tried to step in.

"You can't come with us. We'll take him to Marina Mercy. What's his name?"

One door shut.

Murphy: "Blue."

". . . Yo."

The second door, and skirl rising, the squad went.

Five

On a Sunday morning Dennis Murphy and a bottle woke on a Malinow and Silverman bench at a bus stop. He couldn't tell the time: the sky was grey and indefinite. The Raincheck was up the street but he was 86ed there. He got up and made his way toward the Tropicana and Duke's but stopped at Barney's Beanery.

The Beanery had an aluminum awning the length of it with ribs like a picket fence. The ribs were green and white, the whites very white, and the place looked fresh and clean, waiting for an ocean to overlook and some fish and chips. Rain when it came hit the awning like jumping beans and made it a tympani. In its lee there were neon beer signs along the close-knit windows. Inside was another matter, a bar pool pinball, a maze of rooms. They overlapped one upon another without form or finishing, hand-done. The flooring was rough concrete and uneven; it made you tipsy before your time.

Sunday business was exigent. Early arrivals moored themselves under tiers of old license plates at the bar or found posturepedic wall space beside doorjambs. Elbow power opened watchful watery eyes. Grizzled chins doubled and tripled and broken capillaries rouged many cheeks. Daylight was the bad mood before a bat and it gave way as loads got on. In liquid afternoon they shared the rail as celebrants and soliloquies rose. They were displaced persons but believers: it was why they were here, this water hole, this city and state. They had stories and visions and things to say. Later still the bicker would return.

The man who stood next to Murphy had chewed a cigar stub to phlegm and he began to speak. "Last night," he said, "I ran a snake down and brought up a tree trunk. I went in a hundred feet and still wasn't drawing. I was getting chewing gum, hair balls, Vaseline, and some prophylactics but. Let's get to the root of the matter I said. Right? So I ran the biggest snake I carry down and Bertha, that's what I call her, was rocking and spitting all over the bathroom, like chewing tobacco, not bad, I'll have to remember that, and she was going whang, WHANG, WHA-A-A-AN-NG-NGGGG. I hit a fuckin tap root. The guy's got this deodorant flower sticking out of the back of his toilet and blue water and he's growing trees below. 'What ith it?' he says to me. He's got a lisp and a little friend. I work the Hollywood Hills, otherwise known as the Swish Alps. The two of them are holding each other and moaning about what Bertha is doing to the wallpaper. If you have wallpaper in a bathroom I say you deserve whatever you get, but they're absolutely right. She's making a mess and going WHA-AN-ANG-GGG. This is two or three A.M. I start reelin the snake in. She doesn't want to come. I'm pulling at an anchor. I could be on a charter boat with a marlin on the line. Then up comes Joe Tree, God love it. You should see the thing, it's a wonder the piping's still down there. It must have squeezed in somehow at a fitting point, probably tile piping. I present the fellas with this wig of root. They can't wait to morning to get it unplugged but they don't want anything to do with it. The water's still holding, so I run Bert down partway again and there's some more. Still it's backed up. I wait. I don't know what to do but wait. Then there's this THURRRPP and GLUG and it goes. I had the bathtub full and the pressure builds and THHH-UUU-OOK, a good sound.

"You know, I enjoy plumbing. The pay's pretty good and I

don't mind nights. I like the independence. I've got to call in and go where they tell me, but other than that I'm my own man. I go at my own speed, take my time when I want to. There're rates, but they bend and I charge what I feel's right, and when I'm ready I pack up my van and—*I do it.* I get dirty as hell but what the hell; a shower, a cold beer, several, and— Sometimes I drop in here and air out.

"There's something else, too. I enjoy going into people's houses. I like seeing how different people live, and I see all kinds. Some of them are pretty unbelievable. You see what they're into. Your plumber knows your secrets. They're in the bathroom drains along with the roots. I get to know as much or more than most husbands."

"Take pride in what you do. Take pride," a man beyond the plumber said. He had a staggered stance and ragged teeth and a calculated wild of white hair. He wore overalls and had a brown paper bag in front of him, his solid lunch. "A plumber is an artist of a kind. Ever notice. Try and live in a place and not know the toilet's run, the pipe's song. Houses belch and fart just like people. You're a surgeon of their sounds. You can tell when they're healthy, when they're not. What they're saying. If we're going to live with them we need to keep them healthy. That's the service you're performing. We need you."

"That sounds a little heavy, but thank you very much."

"Coker's my name," the other man said. "And you can't thank people with vision."

"Give a holler if your pipes go. Berta and I will visit you gratis."

The man named Coker said, "You know, the whole universe is sound, the whole universe is language. I'm a student of language and the spoken word. I was other things once. I used to be a carpenter. Forty years ago I was building sets for the picture studios. I liked working with wood and with my hands. It's the same as with a plumber. Woods have smells, you know, pine different from ash or oak. Cut a plank of one and it smells like fresh bread, another might be almost like a woman. There's mystery in the grain and I felt I was touching some of it with my hands. And the capability of building something quick; ah, I liked it. You ever watch different men take hammer and nails? Sometime do it. You can tell by the way they hit their opinion of wood, even in the penny they use. There's a rhythm, and each blow should be clean through, a distinct piece of action.

"But I gave it up. It was slop work. The speed was all that was important to them, so I got another job. For ten years I took care of the sign on the Hollywood mountains. I kept the letters up. At night I'd turn it on—it had lights then—every night until the war began. There was a little house up there where I lived. People would come up to see them and talk to me and once in a while they'd try to take a piece of one or jump off and kill themselves. The old letters are in a bad way now. They're just scrap sheet metal cutouts laid side by side like cards in a football cheering section, with holes in them to let the wind through. I sat up there watching this city grow, the Valley of the Smokes, that's what the Indians and the Spanish called it. I began to take photographs of it. I got to taking one every morning: I have a record of this city for nearly ten years, what each day looked like and how it changed. They may all seem like they're the same, but there're differences. I looked at the letters, too. The sign said HOLLYWOODLAND then, but from where I lived I couldn't see all the letters. I could see the H and the O and a crescent of L. If I moved one way it became an I. They look flat from down here but they're not placed that way. They're on points and in ravines and they jam and disappear. If I moved the other way, down the hill, I could see them all again, the way they coupled and mated, and gradually they revealed themselves to me. I realized I had a gift to give."

"Oh, bullshit," a member of the congregation said placidly. It was something he got to say often.

"Dog squeeze, sheep dip, frog dung, what else? Think of synonyms." The man named Coker adapted without a break to the interruption. "They all have the same construction, two words, really. None quite as satisfactory. The word is pleasing, long and full, then short and to the point. Have you ever noticed how important words have so few letters? Why? They were where we began; they were the first ones and we built around them. Clear day after clear day I studied the H and the O and the L, and then I saw. I grunted them, slurred them and sang them. Do you see, the O and the L, the symbols come from our fingers. Man shaped the letters and then made sounds to fit."

Coker put forefinger to thumb at the nails; then split them perpendicular. He had a bulbous thumb, as if he had missed once too often with his hammer.

"O—L," he said. "Holy. Holly, a cheerful stutter perhaps. I can form almost any word from the hands. I, you, god, love. They are all variations, limbs. But it isn't just English. Om. Woo. I don't care what your secret sound is. We all speak the language. The language of hands precedes all."

The plumber looked askance. "Ten years you were up there?"

Coker nodded.

"Too many clear days can fuck up a guy's head," the man who liked to say bullshit said.

Coker to Murphy: "What do you think?"

Murphy was minding his own solitary business; he was there to be alone without being totally so. He didn't answer, he shrugged.

Coker asked again.

"I don't think," Murphy said, "I don't have any knack for language."

"You're wrong. You see, as you talk to me now you move your hands. Gestures are the real language. What made me start was your hands. Californians have short jabby thumbs-up gestures. Very expressive. You only use one of your hands. The other waits."

Murphy looked at his two hands, tools of trade and thought, and at the bottom of his glass.

Coker said, "There's hand-and-eye coordination and there's hand-and-mouth coordination. More and more of us are nonverbal. But the hands tell." He said, "You're not a Californian?"

"I am."

"You were born here?"

"I've been here twenty-five years, though," Murphy said.

"The war brought you."

"The Navy told me to come."

"But you stayed."

"I hated where I was."

"How come?"

Murphy thought: and thought he knew. He saw with perfect alcoholic and bankrupt lucidity.

He said, "When I was eleven I went to work for my old man. He was a compositor and then his own printer. My mother cut off his shirts at the elbow so he wouldn't have to roll them up, otherwise they'd be totally ruined by ink. Below there, he turned black by the end of the day. He set type. He liked it. He liked very few things but typefaces and he knew their histories. He pottered around with them. Janson, Granjon, Caledonia, a Scotch one. He wanted to find an Irish one. He didn't like large-point type or broad counters with heavy contracts or serifs. Practical faces, no ornaments. And because he knew them I knew them.

He spent all his time working until his eyes weren't any good any longer and I was hired. A dollar seventy-five a day. There was a ceiling lamp that swung and had a green shade, and one light at his working table. Dark other than that. There was hardly a path between the table and the press. The place was in a cellar, a walk-down, a dungeon. The ink smelled like the damp. He was always there except Sundays. Sundays he worked on his car. It was a 1933 Terraplane coupe and he rented a garage to keep it in and he'd take the El over. He hardly ever drove it, but every Sunday he'd work on it and every other Sunday he washed it. It didn't need it but he did it and rubbed the windshields with newspapers after he'd looked them over. He'd go there and not to Mass, but we had to go, and he'd come back for dinner greased instead of inked. It was like a truckdriver's tan. I used to watch the arms when he'd beat me. My mother never saw him except in bed and at breakfast. It didn't matter. She loved the son of a bitch. She was a good Catholic and . . . an alcoholic. She had to have something to do. She had a good education; she'd been going to go to college when she met him. She was proud of his name. She thought she was marrying into some celebrity. The Murphy bed. The guy who came up with it, William Murphy, was my father's second cousin. We were always hearing about him but we never saw him. My mother wanted a brood of sons but didn't get them. She didn't get lots of girls either. The doctors got to know how to do unsuccessful Caesareans on her. There was something wrong with her pelvis. Having children nearly killed her.

"My father had busted out from his family, from Roxbury, Massachusetts, as fast as he could and didn't go back. He made it as far as Chicago, another hellhole. His father, my grandfather, was Roxbury's first trashman and a great swimmer. He swam every day in the summer after work and every Washington's

Birthday he would go into the Atlantic and freeze his balls off. We never got to see him, he and my father didn't speak, but he sent us postcards with doodles on them. He died.

"My father, when he went on his own, printed company papers, school papers, leaflets. Not exactly a big operation. He wanted to but he didn't do very many books. Why go to a lousy printer for that? I didn't want to work for him, that's the only reason he paid me anything at all. I started dropping in a typo or two. I added to drawings, just a line or two. I could draw but wasn't going to let anybody know it. You know. So I'd sketch around the school cartoons. I'd hold them to last setting up. He was sharp but his eyes were going fast. I got away with it, a little thing here, there; but I got tired of it. I started making my own drawings and setting them. I'd stay late or come back at night after a paper was put to bed. I started adding captions to them. And stories. Shit, I loved it. Those little metal chips laid into the chase and racking them. Suddenly—*wack*—they were tight and lined and read right. The drawings were more difficult. You had to sketch them and make a block and an impression. I had discovered girls and I drew some around a story and set it and ran some copies off on yellow paper. I stuck them in the door of the newstand in the middle of the night. The guy circulated them, he didn't throw them out. I did some more, more print, more paper, better drawings. Dirtier. They went too. I was thinking about charging a price when my father caught me. He swept the type off the table. I picked up a handful of type and threw it into his face and he took my left hand in his black two and rammed it into the press."

Murphy said, "He dropped dead at his table in 1945 when I was in Long Beach waiting to be shipped out. I got a pass and went back. He'd fallen into the characters but they'd cleaned him up. He was all pink and white. I watched him, just waiting for him to move so I could tell him what I thought of him. No

goddam Our Fathers. I kept waiting for him to. He seemed to
be just . . . resting. I waited until I saw his cuffs. He had on a
long-sleeve shirt and cufflinks. No ink under his nails. His hands
were clean and I could see the crescent scars from where he'd tried
to deflect the type I'd thrown. And I began to cry."

Murphy stopped awhile, then he said, "The press didn't really
hurt my hand, just broke some veins and capillaries across the
back, no bones." He opened and closed the left hand partway, the
distance it would go. "In 1959 I was in a motorcycle accident and
my hand got crushed. It didn't matter, really. I'd never done
anything more with it anyway."

Coker said, "There was a painter once who lost his hand and
could no longer paint. People kept saying to him how bad it must
be to have lost it, and he said, 'What makes you think I paint
with my hand?' "

"Oh, it still works," Murphy said. "See, here's proof." He
made use of his glass.

"Eighty and eighty-six and ninety proof," the plumber said.

"It's all bullshit anyway," Murphy said.

"I told you so," the bullshitter said.

"The story wasn't true?" the plumber asked. "I missed a few
connections here and there but—"

"Not a word."

"I kind of liked it."

Coker said, "That's not why you came and stayed?"

Murphy shrugged.

"It's the place to come," Coker said. "You got the freedom
to do what you want when you want. Things happen here first,
and the weather's good."

"I came because somebody said to. I wasn't looking for anything."

"That's never true."

"No," Murphy said. "I never had a father and I never came

from anywhere, and I never had a wife. Oh, for a while there was Esther. She thought she was Esther Williams. I thought she was Esther Williams. I thought I was Esther Williams. I used to go down and look at Lake Michigan. It's a cruel piece of water in winter but it didn't matter to me. I used to watch it. You can't swim in it, not there, not anywhere close to there. We swam in Y pools. The walls sweated and rats ran around under the lockers. The water was mostly chlorine. My eyes would puff up after diving. I'd never been in salt water until I came here; it's so thick it's syrup and wraps you up like a life jacket. I could dive. I wasn't a swimmer. I got around, but what I loved was the air and not the water. The things you could do in it. But you needed the water and the board to get into it. I did a back two and a half, a good one. Routine now. You sliced the water, it was barely there. You went in behind your hands straight to toe point. The fingers made almost all the sound. When it was right a *phoosh*. Throw a small rock up and it comes down *pffft*. The body can't do it. A perfect entry makes a small, fast, but slow *phoosh*. When Pat swam she made the sound with her thighs. It was part of her kick and didn't stop. She didn't seem to move in the water. She looked lazy but she cut right through. Oh, Esther."

He said, "I've forgotten her, I don't remember. Never had one."

He said, "She married a Jap. He buys their cars and does business with them. They live in the Valley and everything in the house says MADE IN JAPAN."

"She invites you over often?" the plumber asked.

"I've been there. My sons are there."

"You never had some of them also?"

"Right. The older one's going to college next fall."

"It's fall now."

"Right."

Coker asked, "But what about the motorcycle accident?"

"There I was at forty thousand feet—" Murphy said. "It was a stunt. We were riding scramblers in the desert, light dirt bikes. A hundred and fifteen degrees and we bumped. There was no reason why we did, the road was narrow but straight and freshly tarred. The tar was soft from the heat. It stuck to the tires and to shoes. You could smell it. We had sanded it over. It added as much slipperiness as it subtracted. We were racing: it was the climax. He was the good guy and I was the bad, and there weren't any actors around, they were all through. Just stuntmen and Hell's Angels. The contact was a surprise but just a little kiss, nothing serious, and we parted and stomped it a little and he made his move. I'd been ahead, but he was going to win of course. A good rider, a good man. I spun out, too busy looking at him maybe. Don't know. Everything went out from under. Okay. I let it go, but hesitated. You gotta get off before a bike begins going down, or you don't get off. I had waited and now I was staying. There was no choice. It didn't matter, no big deal. Bruises and scrapes, some stitches, maybe a broken ankle if I didn't get on top, and another take." Murphy said, "But he went off his. I don't know why. He was suddenly off. His bike shot into the cars lined beside the road and ricocheted. I had to dodge it, and there he was. I had my leg free and valuables on top, as much as I could get, and I was planing into him. The wind going by. I put my hand out to the road as a brake and lost the skin. I tried to steer and drag like with a sled. It *did* turn a little. It did turn. Enough, and he rolled the way I turned and I hit him. The fender sliced his head. Flying jello. We slid into the spectators and line of cars and almost hit one, my younger son who was watching and not where he was supposed to be. A friend snatched him up. Blue.

"When we stopped I got up and walked away. Only my hand

got caught and the tendons along the wrist got cut. Otherwise I was fine, just fine.

"But Blue's dead," he said.

"Who? The one you hit?"

But Murphy didn't say. He shut up.

Words—all he'd said and all he wanted to say, the wisdom and the conjugation—weren't solace. They were water through his hands.

He stayed on, quiet Irish, while others began in search of their own.

He got one day's extra work: twenty bucks and a free lunch. He needed them both and wasn't alone. Slowly, before and after the 8:45 A.M. deadline, a hundred or so bodies gathered at the corner of Melrose and Van Ness. The necessary qualifications were sheer need and an ability to hear about the chance and to get there. They waited in the lot next to the Encore Theater, where cars were parked and abandoned, an hour before being divvied into buses which slowly ground through Hollywood and the Cahuenga Pass and then west across the San Fernando Valley and north to Chatsworth, not so far from Sylmar. After the freeways smaller towns came and went, and they passed through orchards and then rocks began to rise, the first foothills. The buses were late but arrived early; the shooting was further behind still. They circled in their own billows and let the sardines loose: the extras fanned out but soon lapped themselves. The location had a hill to climb and some looping rutted roads and dust and nowhere further to go. So they began to wait.

The regulars had the trades. *Buzz buzz.* They picked each squib's bones and traded their own credits, more apocrypha. There were gargoyles among them, waddles and pancake, a cultivated exaggeration that awaited the return of the glory years they hadn't had. But this movie was blaxploitation, and many of the extras were young and handsome and black and full of themselves. They put on a fashion show, slouching hat brims, juking and courting, sensuously bumping through the heat and boredom, as if they might really be noticed. There could have been mirrors at the edges of their peripheral vision.

The shooting fell yet further behind and behind the sun, and the director and crew gave up bothering to match shots. The gaffers leaned against their reflectors and spun them idly, like paddle wheels, and shed their shirts (tucking them into the waistband behind) and lit joints. They waited for action and lunch. Lunch came first.

The menu didn't matter to Murphy, and luckily so—braised chicken and chili, and a vegetable salad of diced beets that squished a watery, royal blood and dyed the dressing and the paper plates. Without bucks he was trying to do without food, without success. Where he could he'd run tabs to the shut-off point. He'd whittled through the canned goods in the Open Road. He knew a free meal at an Episcopal church on Yucca Thursday nights; they opened their doors to anyone. The pickings were lean and he lost weight and his appetite diminished, but not enough. The line moved almost as slowly as the shooting.

"What's your pleasure?" said the girl serving to the crew member ahead of Murphy.

The man's brows bounced. "Let's go off into the bushes and see."

The girl studied the sage and rocks, and laughed. "I'm holding out for a haystack."

"You don't know what you're missing."

She piled up his plate. "Weep for me, and move on," she said.

The man carried his plate to the girl beyond her and took up where he had just left off, the bandy of invitation and innuendo automatic.

The first girl served Murphy.

"Dorie?" Murphy said, a little unsure: her hair had Claireoled from taupe and shortened into a shag; it had reached the cleavage of her buttocks once. In pasted denim and a tie-dyed T with first rhinestones on it, she looked to be the tough up-to-date article.

"Who is it?" She squinted, a recalcitrant myopic.

"Murphy."

No bells. She lowered glasses from her short uneven helmet of hair. They had gradient lenses that muddied the eyes. Still—

"Dennis—"

"Murphy! Is that you? I didn't recognize you. You look . . . different."

"*You* look different."

"I don't know how to take that."

"You look good enough to eat."

"They all say that to me," Dorie Winner (her last name when he had first met her) said, "but I've been doing this for six years now and I don't mind the work. I'm no fool, I take care of myself. There was no one else around to." There was both offense and defense to her stridency. She laughed. "Don't get me started."

She said, "I didn't know you were helping with the stunting. You haven't been here before, have you? I can't see anything anymore."

"It's my first day."

"You must be here for the fight sequence. That's why all the extras are here."

"Right," Murphy said.

"I've got to sling this hash. I'd love to talk to you. You be around?"

"A while." Murphy said.

She came over while he was still sitting down. "So where have you been?" she said. "Et cetera."

"Oh, sneakin by."

"If Jack lets us off, Darla and I will be over to watch the fight." She looked back to Darla still serving: she was Dorie minus years, her clothes were Dorie's minus stones, as tight, as powder-blue. "You know about it, don't you? It's going to start as a fight between the black guy and the white guy but it ends up with everybody in it. The audience gets carried away. Clothes are gonna go too. *Lose* the clothes. That's later, and only a *select* few. Darla and I are thinking about wrestling, be at the bottom of the pile. Can't you see us? If we show our boobies we get fifty extra bucks. I'm outmatched. Darla's got plenty more than that much worth. It's going to be a big jumble of bodies, a group grope, a tasteful orgy. That's what the director says. 'All done in good taste.' " She loved to talk. "They want an R rating, not a PG and not an X. They'd like to shoot an X actually and cut it to an R. That means violence is okay and breasts are okay. I don't know if I'll do it, but if I do, when people see the picture they'll recognize me if they recognize them. That's about all they'll have time to see."

She arched her back, looking herself over, and the rhinestones winked.

"My stars," Murphy said.

Dorie said, "You just might."

"You look fine," Murphy said.

"We keep bobbing along." She said, "You haven't told me what you've been doing."

"Well, I got a new nose."

"Let me see." She touched its new hump and whistled. "I hope Rufe didn't do it to you."

"No."

She said, "How is he?"

Murphy didn't answer a moment.

"What—another horse kick him? Should I send him a card or something. Fat chance. I'm not going to go see him."

"He's dead, Dorie," Murphy said.

The news broke her military perch on the folding chair. "I don't want to know it," she said. "I don't want to hear about it."

"I'm sorry."

"Look, I'm happily married now."

"I'm glad."

"Stop it."

He did.

She said finally, "When?"

"A couple of weeks ago." He shrugged. "A month."

She closed her eyes against the proximity. Slowly each lid grew a salt-water lip amid the heavy Maybelline blades. They broke into the sharp spare lines of wear and tear beside each eye, and she wiped them away.

"There's so much shit," she said. "You try to fight it and forget it but there's no way. Was it sudden?" she asked. "Was he in pain?"

Murphy shook his head. "I don't think he felt a thing."

"Well, tell me about it," she said.

"He . . . we . . . were in a fight and he got hit on the head and had a concussion but seemed really all right. He was up and around and then he passed out one morning and went into a coma. He came out of it once. Janie was the only one there. I don't know if he said anything or not." Murphy said, "A cerebral accident. That's what they called it. Happens every day."

"Always the head. He was probably lucky to have lasted as long as he did."

"The doctors said something like that. There was record of five concussions."

"What about the rest of the kids?"

"They were great. Gail's pregnant, eight months gone and blooming. They flew Chris back from Vietnam."

Dorie shook her head and put it in her hands. She was facing and close to him, stretching bra and bled-blue shirt, a clouded sky. The back ran toward the vanishing point, into the bent center of her. "Chris used to come visit me and he wrote me a letter from Parris Island—is that right? I didn't know how to answer it. I'm no letter writer and it was—*personal.* I hit him at the wrong age. The foolish kid was taken by me. I wrote something back."

Murphy said, "None of the wives was there."

"Oh God," she said. "What a bunch of shits we were. Did he ever get back with that redheaded cow?"

"No."

"That's something at least."

"She wasn't so bad."

"Oh, I know it," Dorie said. "I was the worst. The kid bride who was going to reform the old bandit. Some reformation."

"He wasn't easy to live with."

"For sure. But I could have done better. He never could really take care of himself. I came to think he just wanted Connie back. And all that playing around."

"It didn't mean anything."

"It did to me, probably wouldn't now but it was the world then. I tried to prove it didn't, though, didn't I?"

"What the hell."

"You were nice."

"One of my many mistakes," he said. "The mistake of my life."

"Don't dramatize." She said, "We knew what we were getting into."

"No," Dennis said. "Who ever knows that?"

"Forget it, can't you," she said. "I never told him, he never knew."

"Right."

"The big son of a bitch," Dorie said.

"Dorie," Murphy said.

"It's nothing serious," she said, but the words warped from sudden sob. He touched her clouded sky.

The steel in her soon stopped them and she was soon back helping Darla clean up. She didn't stay for the tasteful orgy, but Murphy sat on until they took the chair from under him and stayed on for the needed, grisly dollars.

The film never made it out of the can.

It was the hottest day of the year and also perfectly clear. The shapes of the land sat up in sharp flat focus like backdrops, and Old Baldy disproved its forty-mile distance and reared a two-dimensional head. The picture window hurt the eyes. The ferocious Santa Ana clarity lacked uric stain and moisture, and at zero humidity woods and wickers crackled like fired kindling, shrinking into themselves. The metal Open Road didn't: it was a dry sauna. Towel nap bristled. The dry degrees itched the skin and nerves. There was no wind, the air was still, carbon monoxide levels soared. There was no comfort.

Murphy had nothing to do, so why get dressed? Any ideas involved energy or money. He hadn't either. Thought alone hurt. He was waiting and waiting for nothing to happen. He turned his radio to blare and tried to sleep. The world would fuzz out but it would return and his fatigue and his deep black agitation grew. Endlessly, he waited for the sun to set. When it came he thought he might be able to find cool, and dress and shuffle off the mortal mood.

He had been alone enough to want to be; a shell had begun to form and toughen. There's a heavy narcotic to loneliness. There was no one he wanted to see, and he didn't want to answer the knock on his door. At first he thought it was an off beat of the radio; even sounds change when you're alone enough, toilets and helicopters, creaks and farts, and finally breathing. Still in his underwear he got up finally, reluctantly in response, and it was Pat.

The sudden sight of her set him back.

She said, "You're here, after all."

"In the flesh."

"So I see."

In front of her the underwear he purposefully hadn't hidden embarrassed him, and that angered him. He growled, "What do you want?"

"Can I come in," she said tightly.

He backed away from the door and picked up shirt and pants and put them on. He turned: she still waited in the bright light. She looked the same and ineffable and slenderer in it. She wore a cotton wraparound skirt and a pale silvery blouse. In the desertlike atmosphere it had the quality of paper flowers. She had on kicked-up brown espadrilles and hoop earrings. Her hair waved despite the weather.

She took a step inside against the light and his hooded look. "Can you turn that noise down?"

He shut the radio off.

She blinked. The heat pressed, the silence hummed. Slowly the swill took shapes in the hot box. She'd been outside but not inside before.

She said, "Do you like it here?"

"I'm happy enough."

"What happened?"

"What do you mean?"

"Where did everything go?"

He looked at the evacuated area. "Oh, I took a few things out. I put in the picture window myself."

"I think you told me." She touched a counter by the door, the remaining kitchenette. There was dust and silt, bugs peddling in the sink.

He said, "The place needs a little cleaning."

"How do you get cockroaches in a trailer?"

"Recreational vehicle," he said. "Where? They're no cockroaches in here."

"What do you call these?"

He looked. "They're not cockroaches. They're . . . bugs."

"The insect expert."

"They must have come in this morning when they heard you were coming."

"I'll bet. How'd they know?"

"There they go. See, they're on their way."

"The first to leave a sinking ship."

"You should know," he said.

Quarrel already. They fell easily quickly always into it and the so many had had effect: in a troubled marriage the insignificant tallies and stores and builds and returns as grudge.

Pat said, "Won't you quit?"

"Me?"

Pat waited, cooling. She said, "I wanted to see how you were."

"Just fine."

"You look terrible."

"Thank you very much."

"You look all ratty and too skinny."

"I do?"

She missed or ignored his meaning. "Yes, and it smells in here. How can you stand it?"

"It's as good as any other place."

"Aren't you doing anything?"

"What is all this shit?"

"I just asked."

"Pick pick pick. It's none of your business what I'm doing. What are you after, more money?"

"What are you talkin about?"

"Alimony or some such."

"I gave up on that long ago."

"It's the only reason I ever get to see you. Dennis, fork it over. Dennis, Pat needs some underwear. Dennis, I need a new girdle" —she never wore girdles—"Dennis, Paul needs some rubbers— prophyLACtics—now that he's going off to college next fall."

"He's there now."

"Oh, that's it. That's what." He was miserably after her.

"That's what what?"

"You're holding that over me. I'm not going to fall for that."

"I'm not holding anything over you."

"Sure," Dennis said. "Back to grub for that money."

"I don't grub, Dennis. I don't grub." Pat was very angry. "The reason I asked was because you said it. And when you did I thought it was important to you."

"I never said it."

"The day the decree became final," Pat said. "Then."

He didn't remember saying it, but the day was the last time she had slept with him. The memory brought pain and then bitter pity: "Throw that up at me."

Pat didn't say anything more awhile. Then she said, "I came because I heard about Rufus. I saw Janie and she told me. She seemed very broken up. She's living in his house at the beach. I wanted to tell you—I wanted you to know that I knew. I wanted to see how you were."

"You see how I am."

"Yes."

"Well, you've scored your points," he said. "Go kiss your rosaries."

"I'm sorry," she said.

"Kiss them," he said in animus, "if you're not still wearing them as a chastity belt."

"Where did that come from?" she said.

"Can't Harold find his way around them?"

"I guess I'd better leave."

"It's about time."

"All right." She put her purse over her shoulder, sick of sniper fire. Turning to go, her effort made, she felt loose of him. Free at last.

But he wasn't, and he threw her against the door. The rattle-clatter of impact wasn't like any wooden door. Her blouse made noise also—when it was touched, it sang with electricity. He kept shaking her and she didn't resist. He needed to get at her. She didn't move.

Even after he stopped he held on to her upper arms, as in wary or weary embrace.

"Is it that you want?" she said.

His hands dropped from the fire.

"What then?"

"I don't know. Nothing. Not a thing."

"Please please please go," he said.

After the door shut Pat stood outside a moment. Going both in and out produced sensations of faint—the brilliance broke down optics. There seemed a semblance of hot moisture inside, but not out. The air chafed the skin. The dryness had no scent but dryness, like wool still on the sheep. The artificial, fecund sweet and sour smells from irrigating semi-arid land were absent. The performance of black spots in front of her eyes came to an end and the Valley and the Basin and the Hollywood sign detached, perfectly discrete. She began to think about thinking again.

She heard him moving inside, crossing the brief geography, tinny feet and a tinny door. She sensed distant moving cars. They were always a presence, an ocean to be heard, and she stood and listened for them, and then she heard the awkward notes of his crying. She listened to them: men shouldn't cry, they don't do it well. They made her feel sorry and strong and freer still. But they didn't stop. The continuing racking sounds were less and less human. They no longer seemed to have relation to tears, after some deeper need. She waited and waited for them to stop. The air hurt her to breathe.

She found him in the bathroom and put a hand to his Airedale hair. "Oh, Denny," she said. "Haven't you anything left?"

He didn't answer and she listened and didn't do anything awhile. Just the cries and his body shaking without rhythm—without salt water. Then she bent and brought his head to her hip. She couldn't go further or do more; they couldn't fit together in the room.

He kept on.

"It's the heat," she said over and over, a sort of croon, "it's the heat, it's the weather. People go a little crazy when it's like this. So damn dry."

She beckoned him out finally, the sounds diminuendo. There he sat. She could leave now, she could leave now; and instead she turned and took him on.

She untied and unwrapped her skirt and let it spin, a subdued Veronica, and with a hand, a high step and a soft sandpaper peel, bared herself below the waist. She left her noisy blouse on and it was a different dark piece inside the Open Road; in stretch and strip it was mercury on the move, and a part of him came alive. She opened to him with a sound like a luff of a sail. The sex was quick, a little ragged. They didn't kiss. The air burned the lungs as they made love.

At the finish her blouse stuck to her at her armpits and at the base of the back. Murphy's hands were there. Sweet sweat. The wetness seemed unguent and without touch the flesh dried. Pat dropped her arms and shoulders and swung her head aside to let the blouse and her bra go—she tossed them away. Then she shucked his underwear. They were bare and her giving and taking blew at his bad weather. Again, and some storm fell away.

He could smell her and taste her. The specifics were watery, elusive, and beyond metaphor. Women's smells. They insinuated in themselves. His hands on her: her detail sustained him. He found places he knew. There were also changes, scalloped spaces, missing weight. In knead there were new textures; her thighs—the gracilis and sartorius didn't jut. Sex isn't flesh and isn't without it. Compare forty and twenty: the hot August when they first met she had unzipped a light pleated skirt and showed them, muscly dunes. They had driven out to Santa Monica with bathing suits beneath their clothes. She undressed the same way then and the sudden maillot racing suit against unsecreted skin and breaking surf was a black plum, like a typewriter ribbon or a new bruise. She worked the swing shift at Lockheed; it ended at midnight and dates regularly began then—the etiquette adjustments for war hadn't rolled back for the postwar boom. She had knotted the ends of her blouse beneath her breasts a second to test the temperature and then it went as well and she kicked off. The Pacific poppled between her thighs. A baby later, Pat pregnant again, they'd returned. Pat waded this time up to her heavied stomach and let her hands wand about her thighs and the skirted bottom of her new white suit, and phosphorescence trailed. He had loved her wet and pregnant.

Lying beside her, he could see a degree of her depletion. Her strength subsided in aftermath. There was grey beneath the tan, mushrooms at dusk. There were rose tongues at the corners of her eyes, fatigue's mascara, and fresh lines of wear and passion softly accordioned. Her eyes were closed but he could see the wet tufts at the other, inside corners, the pink pads: they seemed an intimate part turned out, like a clitoris. A dry bed ran under them and above the bones of her cheeks, new to him. They opened, a wash across her face. In a physical land she had seams showing of days and years.

He spoke to her: "Pablo said you'd been sick."

"Not really. I had a bug."

"More than that," Dennis said.

She opened her eyes. "My son the doctor. It was just some stubborn low-grade infection."

She didn't like to talk about lousy or deepest feelings. She carried health and faith like secrets close to the center of herself.

He said, "You've lost a little weight."

"That never hurts."

"You don't need to. You look good—big."

"Others don't agree."

He re-expressed it with care. "I like you big."

"Well, I look skinny and you look unhappy." Pat said, "So here we are."

She closed her eyes and opened them again, moving herself. She said, "No job now?"

"They come and go still," he said. "Something will happen."

She said, "You're not happy not busy."

"Well, if I wasn't doing this I'd be doing something else."

"Denny."

"What?"

"That's a pile," she said.

"Thanks."

"Know it all," she said about, against herself. "I'm full of wisdom these days. I've gone back to school. I'm taking a course in real estate."

"Are you serious?"

She let the for-sale sign form: "Pat Rhodes and Associates. Another offering of Pat Rhodes and Ass."

"Why?"

"Why what?" She said, "The boys are almost out of the house, you know."

"You'll always be busy."

She said, "I've given up swimming."

"I don't believe that. Some people breathe, you swim."

"After the bug I had—"

"The pneumonia," he said.

"I stopped then," she said. "It wasn't on purpose at first, I was too weak, but now."

"I can't see you sitting around."

"I don't," she said. "They're still meetings, groceries, the thrift shop, the Cabrillo Museum, and the turtle—"

"Horatio Alger's still kicking?"

"Thriving, and of course I'm the one who has to take care of him." She said, "I've also been playing a little tennis."

"Oh Jesus. *Tennis.*"

"I kind of like it."

Murphy said, "Just the right thing for Laguna Beach."

". . . I guess maybe that's so." She said, "I would have told you."

"Eventually."

"Soon eventually." She said, "We've sold the house already."

"At a nice profit, too, knowing him."

"You know I'm not going to talk about him in front of you."

He bit on the easy resentment. "All right. How're things at Santa Cruz? How's he like it?"

"He just loves it. He won't admit it yet. You know, you can't be too enthusiastic. That wouldn't be cool."

"What's he taking?"

"Math and sciences, two physics courses. Beyond me," Pat said.

"Sounds grim."

"He thinks he wants to be an aeronautical engineer."

"You mean he admitted that kind of thing out loud to somebody?"

"Well, not to me," said Pat.

"Oh."

She said, "You ought to see Pat, Dennis. His coach thinks he could make Nationals next year. He's *so* fast. He's under a minute for the hundred fly. Really. Colleges are already after him—S.C., *Indiana, Stanford.* His grades are good."

"He's getting big?" Murphy said.

"Huge."

"How big?"

"He's over six feet."

Much bigger than himself. Dennis said, "Girls are next, look out."

"There's already Teena. She swims freestyle and medley."

"A knockout?"

"Uh-huh."

Pat said, "He won't admit her existence, though, but the evidence's in. He's so quiet and secretive. He won't let any of us in. Maybe Teena, I don't know." She said, "I worry about it."

"But colleges are really after him? That means scholarships. They'll pay him to go."

"I guess."

"I won't have to pay," said Dennis.

She looked at him.

"I never said I'd pay."

"No?" she said, wearied. She knew the song.

"I didn't. I never said that."

"Even last time in May you said you'd do something about it."

"I did not," he said.

"It's time to go," said Pat.

She made to get up and he let loose. He didn't stop her.

She stood akimbo a moment, light between her arms, shoes and earrings on. She hadn't relinquished them. He noticed her again and the chewed foam, the color of toast, where she'd been.

It showed no sign that she had. She began to search for her things. Her hair eddied as she picked them up, short sheaves. A tongue of bush stuck out as she bent over. The clothes had been offered up casually in reaching for him, as throwaways; but they didn't fit back so easily. The skirt wouldn't center, the tie had become unlooped and she had to fish for it, as after an unknotted washing. Finally. Panties then, as she had undressed. She still was naked above the waist, blouse and bra dangling from a hand, crumpled bunting. The added volume of a skirt exaggerated her lost weight. She looked broken, a casualty amid her own pieces.

"There's no subject for us," she said. "There's nothing we can talk safely about."

Then she said, "I thought it might help."

"I told you to go."

He knew his lines; oh he did.

"I know."

"Don't blame me."

"You can't blame someone who won't take blame." She said, "You were drowning. Because of Blue and I don't know what else."

"Bullshit."

"I thought so. I thought you were."

"Well, what the hell then. Let me."

"I didn't want you to."

"Jesus saves."

"Not exactly."

"What then?"

She didn't answer and turned her back to him and reached into her pocketbook. Bad timing: he heard the telling rattle and glimpsed the lasso of beads and was enraged. He ripped the bag out of her hand and hurled it and it hit the picture window like a clapper. The giant pane cobwebbed: lines ran simply and then crackled into intricacy. The light refracted in the cracks, and then in other new ones. The admitted planes danced.

Pat went into the dance and picked up the bag. "I'll be going now."

"You and your goddam beads."

"I was only seeing what time it was," she said, and pulled the string out. Her father's pocket watch—she had inherited it and given it to Murphy, but he hadn't taken it when they had split up—was at the end as well as the twisted figure upon a slender cross. She listened: the watch still ticked.

Murphy said, "What's it doing there?"

"I carry it there."

"Can you do that? They allow it?"

"I don't know. It doesn't matter."

"It doesn't sound like you."

"Let's not talk about me, let's not talk. Let me go in peace," she said.

She began to finish dressing, to get it done. Her blouse moved against the silence.

Push against shove: his rage vanished again in the unsettled debris. Her flesh took cover, and opened him.

"Pat Rhodes Real Estate," he said. "I could offer a listing."

She dressed.

"This," he said. "This here place. This here once-in-a-lifetime ballroom, the dream of all your dreams. For a song, yours for a song, a fucking song. Worth a fortune."

"I'm only taking the course for something to do," Pat said. "Nothing'll come of it."

"Doesn't have to be. You could do it. You'd be good at it. You could move this damn place."

She said, "I don't want it."

"Why not? It's a steal."

"Why do you think not?"

"Bygones be bygones."

"No, they won't," Pat said.

"You know what I mean."

"I do?" She turned to him, last buttoning, tucking in. She put her pocketbook over her shoulder again. "What do you mean?"

"I'm . . . " he said. "Well . . . " he began. "It's like . . ."

She looked at him.

His shoulders moved; his hands opened in supplication. He shrugged he shrugged he shrugged.

"Come see your sons," she said, and a second final time went out the Open Road door.

Pat went to church before going home. She sat in a back pew and bowed her head but didn't kneel. She confessed. She didn't go into the confession box anymore since she had gone ahead with the divorce. Divorced, remarried, she was sure she was ousted. It mattered to her, but her faith survived. Today was a different sort of apostasy. She'd broken her own vows, fucked them away.

Some final bonds had been cut in May: his unwillingness to be pinned down and pay, and she hadn't believed the promise upon her tears. She was sure she could come back now as a person to him, no longer a wife, ex-wife and lover. Be free of that. She'd gone to feel that as well as because of Blue. But seeing him— infrequency only accentuated the pain: there weren't so many viewings to soften the blows. She was less stuck, but her distance made the desolation harder not to see. So she had given of what he had called her squeaky self.

What is once out of a lifetime anyway? The first time you make love, perhaps, but at this point? It could be everything, couldn't it. She knew that but not what it would daily mean.

For twenty years he had jumped in her head on a diving board, counting the steps to the end and testing the spring, gathering bounce. Using the board's leverage. The time she had watched he hadn't dived, but come to a stop and begun again. He did still, the dark prince of her life. She carried that vision, and other quick snaps; she still didn't know why she remembered the little as lastingly as the consequential; some way off the bone bled through her life with the stealth of dream and a measure of infinity.

Pat let the natant memories take hold. For her, water had always offered a salutary effect. She remembered the muggy smell of Visalia pools, sweet armpits and hot radiators; with moisture in it the Open Road would have been kin. Dennis had been right about her love of it.

She would swim once again, but she couldn't finally measure what she'd done. It was done done done. No tears. Silent prayer and a Gloria Patri. Her forehead met the pew, and when she arose a mark was left where it had touched, like Lenten ash; and she went home to her husband and her sons, home and away, to a stepdaughter and a turtle, her family, and began preparing for the coming of the moving vans.

After Pat left, Murphy waited for a weather change. The skin felt it first when it finally came and the sky became lightly smeared, a consommé. Tomorrow would be normal: hot and clear and dry but not as dry. At sunset the west-facing hills turned bisque to roan. The world was beautiful for five minutes. The look of laterite didn't last, the shade withdrew, the hills lost the sun and then the light. They took on brooding bulk. On other regular days dusk brought a little clarity briefly back.

In ones and twos the streetlights came on. A lazy complexing question came out of them down the canyon and up the far side, then less simple shapes. They piled in the basin without such consideration. Night arrived. The sky wasn't dark—it was a restless grey nimbus, a sign of fall, and reflected light. The weather would eventually cool and in December there might be rain.

If it came, there would be little rinsing sadness to it. It would drown the earth. The hills would shed houses like clothes and the air would fill with a peculiar fertility. Smells would resume and prosper, sweet and fecal. And then the normal atmosphere would return to stay indefinitely.

His cracked window puzzled the changing pigmentations. They seemed to move transiently piece to piece, migrant shades. They were in turn like bands of a dying rainbow, and with Pat still in the air Murphy fell asleep in the driver's seat. He didn't wake until morning and then he went down the hill and put his land on the market and sold the Open Road. He sent the money on to his sons and talked his way back into garbaging for a while.